The Science-Based Anti-Inflammatory
Diet Cookbook for Beginners

1800 Dyas Delicious and Nutritious Anti-Inflammatory Recipes with a 30-Day Meal Plan to Reduce Inflammation and Enhance Immunity

Lucilla J. Simmons

CONTENTS

Soups & Stews 72

Introduction

My name is Lucilla J. Simmons, and I am excited to introduce you to my latest cookbook, The Science-Based Anti-Inflammatory Diet Cookbook for Beginners: 1800 Days Delicious and Nutritious Anti-Inflammatory Recipes with a 30-Day Meal Plan to Reduce Inflammation and Enhance Immunity. As a certified nutritionist and health coach, I have dedicated my career to helping people achieve optimal health through diet and lifestyle changes. This cookbook is the culmination of years of research, experimentation, and passion for healthy living.

I wrote this cookbook because I believe that food is medicine. Inflammation is a root cause of many chronic diseases, including arthritis, heart disease, and cancer. As a result, reducing inflammation through diet is a crucial component of preventing and managing these conditions. Unfortunately, many people are not aware of the anti-inflammatory properties of certain foods or how to incorporate them into their diets. I wanted to create a cookbook that would make it easy and enjoyable for people to eat delicious, anti-inflammatory meals and improve their health.

The Science-Based Anti-Inflammatory Diet Cookbook for Beginners is not just a collection of recipes - it's a comprehensive guide to reducing inflammation and enhancing immunity through diet. The book includes 1800 days' worth of recipes for breakfast, lunch, dinner, and snacks, all carefully crafted to be both delicious and nutritious. Each recipe features whole, unprocessed foods that are rich in anti-inflammatory nutrients, such as omega-3 fatty acids, antioxidants, and fiber. In addition, the book includes a 30-day meal plan designed to help readers get started on a path to better health.

Moreover, this cookbook is not just for people who are dealing with inflammation-related health issues. It's for anyone who wants to improve their overall health and wellbeing. The recipes in this book are designed to be enjoyable and satisfying, with a wide variety of flavors and cuisines represented. Whether you're a seasoned cook or a beginner, you'll find recipes that are easy to make and that will impress your family and friends.

By following the recipes in this book, you can reduce inflammation, boost your immunity, and enjoy delicious and nutritious meals. So don't wait any longer - get your copy today and start your journey towards a healthier, happier lifestyle today!

What is the Anti-Inflammatory Diet exactly?

The anti-inflammatory diet is a type of eating plan that focuses on foods that have anti-inflammatory properties, while avoiding foods that cause inflammation in the body. Inflammation is a natural response of the body's immune system to injury or infection. However, chronic inflammation has been linked to a variety of health problems, including heart disease, diabetes, cancer, and arthritis.

The anti-inflammatory diet aims to reduce chronic inflammation in the body, which can improve overall health and reduce the risk of chronic diseases.

What are the health benefits of following a Anti-Inflammatory Diet?

Following an anti-inflammatory diet has been associated with a variety of health benefits. Chronic inflammation has been linked to a range of health problems, including heart disease, diabetes, cancer, and arthritis. The anti-inflammatory diet aims to reduce chronic inflammation in the body by including foods that have anti-inflammatory properties and avoiding foods that cause inflammation. Here are some of the health benefits of following an anti-inflammatory diet:

- **Reduced Risk of Chronic Diseases**

Following an anti-inflammatory diet can reduce the risk of chronic diseases such as heart disease, diabetes, cancer, and arthritis. Chronic inflammation has been linked to the development of these diseases, and reducing inflammation in the body can help prevent and manage them.

- **Improved Heart Health**

The anti-inflammatory diet includes foods that are low in saturated fat and high in healthy fats, such as omega-3 fatty acids, which can improve heart health. These foods can help reduce blood pressure, lower cholesterol levels, and prevent the buildup of plaque in the arteries.

- **Improved Gut Health**

The anti-inflammatory diet includes high-fiber foods that can improve gut health by promoting the growth of beneficial gut bacteria. This can help improve digestion, reduce inflammation in the gut, and improve overall health.

- **Reduced Pain and Inflammation**

Following an anti-inflammatory diet can reduce pain and inflammation associated with conditions such as rheumatoid arthritis, osteoarthritis, and other inflammatory conditions. The diet includes foods that have anti-inflammatory properties, such as fruits, vegetables, whole grains, and healthy fats, which can help reduce inflammation in the body.

- **Improved Mental Health**

The anti-inflammatory diet has also been associated with improved mental health. Chronic inflammation has been linked to depression, anxiety, and other mental health conditions. The diet includes foods that are high in antioxidants and vitamins, which can improve brain function and reduce the risk of these conditions.

● **Weight Loss**

The anti-inflammatory diet is also associated with weight loss. The diet includes high-fiber foods that help keep you full and reduce cravings for unhealthy foods. It also includes healthy fats and lean protein, which can help build muscle and burn fat.

What foods should be limited or avoided on the Anti-Inflammatory Diet?

To reduce chronic inflammation in the body, it is important to limit or avoid certain foods. Here are some of the foods that should be limited or avoided on the anti-inflammatory diet:

● **Processed Foods**

Processed foods such as fast food, snacks, and sugary drinks are high in sugar, salt, and unhealthy fats, which can cause inflammation in the body. These foods should be avoided or limited as much as possible.

● **Trans Fats**

Trans fats, which are found in fried foods, processed snacks, and baked goods, are particularly harmful and should be avoided. They have been linked to a variety of health problems, including heart disease and inflammation.

● **Red Meat**

Red meat is high in saturated fat, which can increase inflammation in the body. It is recommended to limit your consumption of red meat and choose lean protein sources such as chicken, turkey, and fish instead.

● **Refined Carbohydrates**

Refined carbohydrates such as white bread, pasta, and white rice are low in fiber and can cause inflammation in the body. Substitute them with whole grains such as brown rice, quinoa, and whole wheat which are rich in fiber and help to reduce inflammation in the body.

● **Sugary Drinks**

Sugary drinks such as soda and sports drinks are high in sugar and can cause inflammation in the body. They should be avoided or limited as much as possible. Instead, opt for water, herbal tea, or unsweetened beverages.

● **Alcohol**

Alcohol can cause inflammation in the body and should be consumed in moderation. It is recommended to limit your alcohol intake to one drink per day for women and two drinks per day for men.

● **Saturated and Trans Fats**

Saturated fats, which are found in animal products such as butter, cheese, and fatty meats, can increase inflammation in the body. Trans fats, which are found in fried foods, processed snacks, and baked goods, are particularly harmful. It is recommended to limit your intake of saturated and trans fats and choose healthy fats such as olive oil, nuts, and seeds instead.

How to get started with a Anti-Inflammatory Diet?

Getting started with an anti-inflammatory diet can seem daunting, but with a few simple steps, it can be a manageable and delicious way of eating. Here are some tips for getting started with an anti-inflammatory diet:

- **Learn the Basics**

Before you start an anti-inflammatory diet, it's important to learn the basics of what foods to include and what foods to avoid. As we have discussed earlier, the anti-inflammatory diet involves consuming whole, nutrient-dense foods that have anti-inflammatory properties, while avoiding or limiting processed and inflammatory foods.

- **Make a Plan**

Start by making a plan of what foods you will eat and what foods you will avoid. Plan your meals and snacks ahead of time to ensure that you have healthy options available.

- **Incorporate More Fruits and Vegetables**

Fruits and vegetables are high in fiber, vitamins, minerals, and antioxidants, which help to reduce inflammation in the body. Aim to incorporate more fruits and vegetables into your meals and snacks.

- **Choose Healthy Fats**

Healthy fats such as olive oil, nuts, seeds, and fatty fish are high in omega-3 fatty acids and have anti-inflammatory properties. Choose healthy fats to replace unhealthy fats such as saturated and trans fats.

- **Cook at Home**

Cooking at home allows you to control the ingredients and ensure that you are consuming whole, nutrient-dense foods. Experiment with new recipes that incorporate anti-inflammatory foods.

- **Read Labels**

When shopping for food, read labels to ensure that you are choosing foods that are low in sugar, salt, and unhealthy fats, and high in fiber and nutrients. Avoid processed foods that contain a lot of additives and preservatives.

- **Stay Hydrated**

Drinking plenty of water can help reduce inflammation in the body. Make sure to stay hydrated throughout the day by drinking water, herbal tea, or unsweetened beverages.

- **Be Patient**

It takes time for your body to adjust to a new way of eating. Be patient and don't expect to see results overnight. Stick with the anti-inflammatory diet and you will begin to notice the benefits over time.

Breakfast And Brunch

Granola Dish With Buckwheat, Berries, Apples, Pumpkin Seeds And Sunflower Seeds

Servings: 2

Cooking Time: 45 Minutes

Ingredients:

- 1 cup oats, whole meal or steel cut
- ⅓ cup buckwheat
- 2 cups water
- ⅓ cup sunflower seeds
- ⅓ cup pumpkin seeds
- ⅓ cup strawberries or raspberries, chopped
- ½ cup apples, peeled and finely chopped
- 5 tablespoon coconut oil
- 4 tablespoon cacao powder

Directions:

1. Preheat the oven to 350°F.
2. Into a bowl mix the oats, buckwheat, and seeds.
3. For 10 to 15 minutes, put the berries, apples, coconut oil and water in a pan. Then cover and simmer on a medium-high heat until the fruits are soft and stir in the ginger.
4. In a blender, add the fruit mixture with the cacao then blend until smooth. With the buckwheat, mix the fruits.
5. Use coconut oil to grease the baking tray and spread the granola mixture using a knife or spatula on top to create a thin layer. Bake for 45 minutes.
6. Every 15 minutes, stir the mixture so it doesn't burn. Remove the tray when crispy all over and allow to cool.

Nutrition Info:

- Info Per Serving: Calories: 780| Fat: 59g ;Protein: 22g ;Carbs: 69g .

Mediterranean Coconut Pancakes

Servings: 4

Cooking Time: 5 Minutes

Ingredients:

- 4 eggs
- 1 cup coconut or almond milk, plus additional as needed
- 1 tablespoon melted coconut oil, or almond butter, plus additional
- 1 tablespoon maple syrup
- 1 teaspoon vanilla extract
- ½ cup coconut flour
- 1 teaspoon baking soda
- ½ teaspoon sea salt

Directions:

1. Mix together the eggs, coconut milk, coconut oil, maple syrup, and vanilla in a medium bowl with an electric mixer.
2. Stir together the coconut flour, baking soda, and salt in a small bowl. Add these dry ingredients to the wet ingredients and beat well, until smooth and lump free.
3. Add additional liquid to thin to the consistency of traditional pancake batter if the batter is too thick.
4. Lightly grease a large skillet with coconut oil. Place it over medium-high heat.
5. Add the batter in ½-cup scoops and cook for about 3 minutes, or until golden brown on the bottom. Flip and cook for about 2 minutes more.
6. Stack the pancakes on a plate and continue to cook the remaining batter which makes about 8 pancakes.

Nutrition Info:

- Info Per Serving: Calories: 193 ;Fat: 11g ;Protein: 9g ;Carbs: 15g .

Scrambled Eggs With Smoked Salmon

Servings: 4

Cooking Time: 15 Minutes

Ingredients:

- 2 chopped chives, chopped
- 2 tbsp olive oil
- 6 oz smoked salmon, flaked
- 8 eggs, beaten
- ¼ tsp ground black pepper

Directions:

1. Warm the olive oil in a skillet over medium heat and cook the salmon for 3 minutes, stirring often. Beat the eggs and pepper in a bowl, pour it over the salmon, and cook for 5 minutes, stirring gently until set. Top with chives and serve warm.

Nutrition Info:

- Info Per Serving: Calories: 240;Fat: 19g;Protein: 17g;Carbs: 1g.

Baked Berry Millet With Applesauce

Servings: 6
Cooking Time: 65 Minutes
Ingredients:

- 2 cups blueberries
- 1 cup millet
- 2 cups sugar-free applesauce
- ⅓ cup coconut oil, melted
- 2 tsp grated fresh ginger
- 1 ½ tsp ground cinnamon

Directions:

1. Place your oven to 350ºF. Mix the millet, blueberries, applesauce, coconut oil, ginger, and cinnamon in a large bowl. Pour the mixture into a casserole dish. Cover with aluminum foil. Bake for 40 minutes. Remove the foil and bake for 10-15 minutes more until lightly crisp on top.

Nutrition Info:

- Info Per Serving: Calories: 325;Fat: 14g;Protein: 6g;Carbs: 48g.

Simple Apple Muffins

Servings: 6
Cooking Time: 40 Minutes
Ingredients:

- 1 egg
- 2 cups whole-wheat flour
- 1 cup pure date sugar
- 2 tsp baking powder
- ¼ tsp sea salt
- 2 tsp cinnamon powder
- 1/3 cup melted coconut oil
- 1/3 cup almond milk
- 2 apples, chopped
- ½ cup almond butter, cubed

Directions:

1. Preheat your oven to 400ºF. Grease 6 muffin cups with cooking spray. In a bowl, mix 1 ½ cups of whole-wheat flour, ¾ cup of the date sugar, baking powder, salt, and 1 tsp of cinnamon powder. Whisk in the melted coconut oil, egg, and almond milk and fold in the apples. Fill the muffin cups two-thirds way up with the batter.

2. In a bowl, mix the remaining flour, remaining date sugar, and cold almond butter. Top the muffin batter with the mixture. Bake for 20 minutes. Remove the muffins onto a wire rack, allow cooling, and dust them with the remaining cinnamon powder. Serve and enjoy!

Nutrition Info:

- Info Per Serving: Calories: 463;Fat: 18g;Protein: 8.2g;Carbs: 71g.

Almond Flour English Muffins

Servings: 4
Cooking Time: 20 Minutes
Ingredients:

- 2 eggs
- 2 tbsp almond flour
- ½ tsp baking powder
- 1 pinch of sea salt
- 3 tbsp peanut butter

Directions:

1. In a bowl, combine the almond flour, baking powder, and salt. Then, pour in the eggs and whisk. Let the batter sit for 5 minutes to set. Melt the peanut butter in a frying pan and add the mixture in four dollops. Fry until golden brown on one side, then flip the bread with a spatula and fry further until golden brown. Serve.

Nutrition Info:

- Info Per Serving: Calories: 123;Fat: 9.2g;Protein: 6.5g;Carbs: 3.5g.

Pear & Kale Smoothie

Servings: 2
Cooking Time: 5 Minutes
Ingredients:

- 3 cups baby kale
- ¼ cup cilantro leaves
- 2 pears, peeled and chopped
- 2 cups sugar-free apple juice
- 1 tbsp grated ginger
- 1 cup crushed ice

Directions:

1. Place the kale, cilantro, pears, apple juice, ginger, and ice in a food processor and pulse until smooth. Serve.

Nutrition Info:

- Info Per Serving: Calories: 310;Fat: 2g;Protein: 2g;Carbs: 78g.

Berry Quinoa Bowl

Servings: 4
Cooking Time: 5 Minutes
Ingredients:

- 3 cups cooked quinoa
- 2 cups almond milk
- 2 bananas, sliced
- 2 cups berries
- ½ cup chopped hazelnuts

- ¼ cup maple syrup

Directions:

1. In a large bowl, combine the quinoa, milk, banana, raspberries, blueberries, and hazelnuts. Divide between serving bowls and top with maple syrup to serve.

Nutrition Info:

- Info Per Serving: Calories: 960;Fat: 42g;Protein: 23g;Carbs: 128g.

Scrambled Tofu With Bell Pepper

Servings: 4
Cooking Time: 20 Minutes
Ingredients:

- 2 tbsp olive oil
- 1 firm tofu, crumbled
- 1 red bell pepper, chopped
- 1 green bell pepper, chopped
- 1 tomato, finely chopped
- 2 chopped green onions
- Sea salt and pepper to taste
- 1 tsp turmeric powder
- 1 tsp Creole seasoning
- ½ cup chopped baby kale
- ¼ cup grated Parmesan

Directions:

1. Warm the olive oil in a skillet over medium heat and add the tofu. Cook with occasional stirring until the tofu is light golden brown while making sure not to break the tofu into tiny bits but to have scrambled egg resemblance, 5 minutes. Stir in the bell peppers, tomato, green onions, salt, pepper, turmeric powder, and Creole seasoning. Sauté until the vegetables soften, 5 minutes. Mix in the kale to wilt, 3 minutes and then half of the Parmesan cheese. Allow melting for 1-2 minutes and then turn the heat off. Top with the remaining cheese and serve.

Nutrition Info:

- Info Per Serving: Calories: 159;Fat: 11g;Protein: 10g;Carbs: 7.1g.

Fruity And Seedy Breakfast Bars

Servings: 6
Cooking Time: 30 Minutes
Ingredients:

- ½ cup dates, pitted
- ¾ cup sunflower seeds, toasted
- ¾ cup pumpkin seeds, toasted
- ¾ cup white sesame seeds
- ½ cup blueberries, dried
- ½ cup cherries, dried

- ¼ cup flaxseed
- ½ cup almond butter

Directions:

1. Preheat the oven to 325°F.
2. Using a parchment paper, line an 8-by-8-inch baking dish.
3. Pulse the dates in a food processor until chopped into a paste.
4. Add the sunflower seeds, pumpkin seeds, sesame seeds, blueberries, cherries, and flaxseed, and pulse to combine then scoop the mixture into a medium bowl.
5. Stir in the almond butter. Transfer the mixture to the prepared dish and press it down firmly.
6. Bake for about 30 minutes, or until firm and golden brown.
7. Cool for about 1 hour, until it is at room temperature. Remove from the baking dish and cut into 12 squares.
8. Refrigerate in a sealed container for up to 1 week.

Nutrition Info:

- Info Per Serving: Calories: 312 ;Fat: 4g ;Protein: 10g;Carbs:22 g .

Flaky Eggs With Cabbage

Servings: 1
Cooking Time: 10 Minutes
Ingredients:

- 1 tablespoon coconut oil or avocado oil
- ½ medium head cabbage, sliced
- 2 slices prosciutto, ham, or bacon
- 2 large eggs
- ½ teaspoon fine Himalayan salt

Directions:

1. Heat an 8-inch skillet or griddle over medium heat. Melt the oil in the skillet when it's hot and swirl it around to grease the entire surface.
2. Add the cabbage, distributing it evenly over the whole skillet in one even layer. Let it cook undisturbed until the bottom of the cabbage browns for 5 minutes. Form a little mound by moving the cabbage to one side of the skillet.
3. On the other side of the skillet, put the prosciutto slices and cook for 2 to 3 minutes until crispy then flip it once. Then push the prosciutto to the side, snuggled up against the cabbage.
4. Into the remaining space in the skillet, crack the eggs and sprinkle everything with salt. For 2 to 3 minutes, let the eggs cook until the whites are no longer translucent and has crispy edges. Use a spatula to gently distribute the loose egg white over the cooked egg parts if the eggs look done except

for little pools of raw white near the yolk, until they too are cooked.

Nutrition Info:

- Info Per Serving: Calories: 437 ;Fat: 33.6g ;Protein: 30.4g;Carbs: 8.7g .

Blueberry Muesli Breakfast

Servings: 4
Cooking Time: 10 Minutes

Ingredients:

- 2 cups spelt flakes
- 2 cups puffed cereal
- ¼ cup sunflower seeds
- ¼ cup almonds
- ¼ cup raisins
- ¼ cup dried cranberries
- ¼ cup chopped dried figs
- ¼ cup shredded coconut
- ¼ cup dark chocolate chips
- 3 tsp ground cinnamon
- ½ cup coconut milk
- ½ cup blueberries

Directions:

1. In a bowl, combine the spelt flakes, puffed cereal, sunflower seeds, almonds, raisins, cranberries, figs, coconut, chocolate chips, and cinnamon. Toss to mix well. Pour in the coconut milk. Let sit for 1 hour and serve topped with blueberries.

Nutrition Info:

- Info Per Serving: Calories: 333;Fat: 15g;Protein: 6.2g;Carbs: 49g.

Almond & Coconut Granola With Cherries

Servings: 6
Cooking Time: 45 Minutes

Ingredients:

- ½ cup coconut oil, melted
- ½ cup maple syrup
- 1 tsp vanilla extract
- 3 tsp pumpkin pie spice
- 4 cups rolled oats
- ⅓ cup whole-wheat flour
- ¼ cup ground flaxseed
- ½ cup sunflower seeds
- ½ cup slivered almonds
- ½ cup shredded coconut
- ½ cup dried cherries

- ½ cup dried apricots, chopped

Directions:

1. Preheat your oven to 350ºF. In a bowl, combine the coconut oil, maple syrup, and vanilla. Add in the pumpkin pie spice. Put oats, flour, flaxseed, sunflower seeds, almonds, and coconut on a baking sheet and toss to combine. Coat with the oil mixture. Spread the granola out evenly. Bake for 25 minutes. Once ready, break the granola into chunks and stir in the cherries and apricots. Bake another 5 minutes. Allow cooling and serve.

Nutrition Info:

- Info Per Serving: Calories: 585;Fat: 32g;Protein: 12g;Carbs: 66.2g.

Cherry Oatmeal

Servings: 2
Cooking Time: 15 Minutes

Ingredients:

- 1 cup almond milk
- A pinch of sea salt
- 1 cup old-fashioned oats
- ½ cup dried cherries, pitted
- 1 tsp ground cinnamon

Directions:

1. Place the almond milk, 1 cup of water, and salt in a pot over high heat and bring to a boil. Mix in oats, cherries, and cinnamon, lower the heat, and simmer for 5 minutes, stirring occasionally. Turn the heat off and let sit covered for 3 minutes. Serve warm.

Nutrition Info:

- Info Per Serving: Calories: 491;Fat: 32g;Protein: 4g;Carbs: 49g.

Raspberry Almond Smoothie

Servings: 4
Cooking Time: 5 Minutes

Ingredients:

- 1 ½ cups almond milk
- ½ cup raspberries
- Juice from half lemon
- ½ tsp almond extract

Directions:

1. In a blender or smoothie maker, pour the almond milk, raspberries, lemon juice, and almond extract. Puree the ingredients at high speed until the raspberries have blended almost entirely into the liquid. Pour the smoothie into serving glasses. Stick in some straws. Serve.

Nutrition Info:

- Info Per Serving: Calories: 217;Fat: 21g;Protein: 2.2g;Carbs: 6.9g.

Dilly Vegetable Quinoa

Servings: 1
Cooking Time: 25 Minutes
Ingredients:
- ½ broccoli head, chopped
- ¼ cup quinoa
- 1 carrot, grated
- ¼ tsp sea salt
- 1 tbsp chopped fresh dill

Directions:
1. Stir the quinoa and ¾ cup water in a pot over high heat. Bring to a boil. Reduce the heat to low. Cover and cook for 5 minutes. Add the broccoli, carrot, and salt. Cook for 10-12 minutes more, or until the quinoa is fully cooked and tender. If the stew gets too dry, add more water. This should be on the liquid side, as opposed to the drier consistency of a pilaf. Fold in the dill and serve.

Nutrition Info:
- Info Per Serving: Calories: 220;Fat: 3g;Protein: 10g;Carbs: 42g.

Strawberry & Pecan Breakfast

Servings: 2
Cooking Time: 15 Minutes
Ingredients:
- 1 can coconut milk, refrigerated overnight
- 1 cup granola
- ½ cup pecans, chopped
- 1 cup sliced strawberries

Directions:
1. Drain the coconut milk liquid. Layer the coconut milk solids, granola, and strawberries in small glasses. Top with chopped pecans and serve right away.

Nutrition Info:
- Info Per Serving: Calories: 644;Fat: 79g;Protein: 23g;Carbs: 82g.

Coconut Oat Bread

Servings: 4
Cooking Time: 50 Minutes
Ingredients:
- 4 cups whole-wheat flour
- ¼ tsp sea salt
- ½ cup rolled oats
- 1 tsp baking soda
- 1 ¾ cups coconut milk, thick

- 2 tbsp pure maple syrup

Directions:
1. Preheat your oven to 450ºF. In a bowl, mix flour, salt, oats, and baking soda. Add in coconut milk and maple syrup and whisk until dough forms. Dust your hands with some flour and knead the dough into a ball. Shape the dough into a circle and place on a baking sheet.
2. Cut a deep cross on the dough and bake in the oven for 15 minutes. Reduce the heat to 400ºF and bake further for 20-25 minutes or until a hollow sound is made when the bottom of the bread is tapped. Slice and serve.

Nutrition Info:
- Info Per Serving: Calories: 761;Fat: 27g;Protein: 17g;Carbs: 115g.

Kale & Avocado Toast

Servings: 1
Cooking Time:10 Minutes
Ingredients:
- 1 halved avocado, pitted
- 2 gluten-free bread slices
- 1 tbsp lemon juice
- Sea salt to taste
- 2 cups spinach

Directions:
1. Steam the spinach for approximately 4 minutes or until wilted. Into a small bowl, scoop the avocado flesh from the peel with a spoon. Add the lemon juice and salt. Mash together with a fork. Taste and adjust the seasoning with more lemon juice and salt. Toast the bread. Divide the avocado mixture between the two pieces of toast. Top each with half of the wilted spinach. Serve and enjoy!

Nutrition Info:
- Info Per Serving: Calories: 590;Fat: 45g;Protein: 6g;Carbs: 46g.

Maple Crêpes

Servings: 2
Cooking Time: 15 Minutes
Ingredients:
- ½ cup almond milk
- 2 eggs
- 1 tsp vanilla
- 1 tsp pure maple syrup
- 1 cup whole-wheat flour
- 3 tbsp coconut oil

Directions:
1. Combine the eggs, vanilla, almond milk, ½ cup of water, and syrup in a mixing bowl. Add the flour to the mix and

whisk to combine to a smooth paste. Take 2 tablespoons of the coconut oil and melt in a pan over medium heat. Add ½ crepe mixture and tilt and swirl the pan to form a round crepe shape. Cook for about 2 minutes until the bottom is light brown and comes away from the pan with the spatula. Flip and cook for 2 minutes. Repeat with the rest of the mixture. Serve and enjoy!

Nutrition Info:

- Info Per Serving: Calories: 615;Fat: 40g;Protein: 13g;Carbs: 54g.

Sweet Potato, Tomato, & Onion Frittata

Servings: 4

Cooking Time: 30 Minutes

Ingredients:

- 6 large eggs, beaten
- 1 tomato, chopped
- ¼ cup almond milk
- 1 tbsp tomato paste
- 1 tbsp olive oil
- 2 tbsp coconut flour
- 5 tbsp chopped onion
- 1 tsp minced garlic clove
- 2 shredded sweet potatoes

Directions:

1. Whisk the wet ingredients together in a bowl. Fold in the dry ingredients and stir to combine well. Place the mixture in a baking dish that will fit into the Instant Pot. Place a trivet in the pressure cooker and pour 1 cup of water inside. Place the baking dish in your pressure cooker on top of the trivet. Seal the lid and turn the sealing vent to "sealing". Cook for 18 minutes on "Manual" on High pressure. Once completed, let the pressure release naturally for 10 minutes and serve hot. Enjoy!

Nutrition Info:

- Info Per Serving: Calories: 190;Fat: 11g;Protein: 11g;Carbs: 12g.

Mushroom Crepes

Servings: 4

Cooking Time: 25 Minutes

Ingredients:

- 1 cup whole-wheat flour
- 1 tsp onion powder
- ½ tsp baking soda
- ¼ tsp sea salt
- 1 cup crumbled tofu
- ⅓ cup almond milk

- ¼ cup lemon juice
- 2 tbsp extra-virgin olive oil
- ½ cup chopped mushrooms
- ½ cup finely chopped onion
- 2 cups collard greens

Directions:

1. Combine the flour, onion powder, baking soda, and salt in a bowl. Place the tofu, almond milk, lemon juice, and oil in your food processor. Blitz until everything is well combined. Add to the the flour mixture and mix to combine. Stir in mushrooms, onion, and collard greens.

2. Heat a skillet and grease with cooking spray. Lower the heat and spread a ladleful of the batter across the surface of the skillet. Cook for 4 minutes on both sides or until set. Remove to a plate. Repeat the process until no batter is left, greasing with a little more oil, if needed. Serve.

Nutrition Info:

- Info Per Serving: Calories: 282;Fat: 15g;Protein: 10g;Carbs: 30g.

Thyme Cremini Oats

Servings: 4

Cooking Time: 30 Minutes

Ingredients:

- 8 oz cremini mushrooms, sliced
- 14 oz chicken broth
- ½ onion, diced
- 2 tbsp olive oil
- 1 cup steel-cut oats
- 3 thyme sprigs
- 2 garlic cloves, minced
- Sea salt and pepper to taste

Directions:

1. Heat the olive oil in your pressure cooker on "Sauté". Add onion and mushrooms and sauté for 3 minutes. Add the garlic and sauté for one minute more. Stir in the oats and cook for an additional minute. Pour in ½ of water, broth, and add thyme sprigs. Season with some salt and pepper. Seal the lid and cook on "Manual" on High for 12 minutes. Once completed, let the pressure release naturally for 10 minutes, then perform a quick pressure release. Serve immediately and enjoy!

Nutrition Info:

- Info Per Serving: Calories: 270;Fat: 13g;Protein: 9g;Carbs: 30g.

Delicious Matcha Smoothie

Servings: 4
Cooking Time: 5 Minutes
Ingredients:
- 1 cup chopped pineapple
- 1 cup chopped mango
- 1 cup chopped spinach
- ½ avocado
- ½ cup almond milk
- 1 tsp matcha powder

Directions:
1. Purée everything in a blender until smooth, adding 1 cup water if needed. In a food processor, place the pineapple, mango, spinach, avocado, almond milk, water, and matcha powder. Blitz until smooth. Serve in glasses.

Nutrition Info:
- Info Per Serving: Calories: 168;Fat: 12g;Protein: 2g;Carbs: 16.1g.

Tropical Smoothie Bowl

Servings: 4
Cooking Time: 10 Minutes
Ingredients:
- 4 bananas, sliced
- 1 cup papaya, chopped
- 1 cup granola, crushed
- 2 cups fresh raspberries
- ½ cup slivered almonds
- 4 cups coconut milk

Directions:
1. Put bananas, raspberries, and coconut milk in a food processor and pulse until smooth. Transfer to a bowl and stir in granola. Top with almonds. Serve and enjoy!

Nutrition Info:
- Info Per Serving: Calories: 840;Fat: 78g;Protein: 19.3g;Carbs: 86g.

Appetizing Crepes With Berries

Servings: 4 To 6
Cooking Time: 5 Minutes
Ingredients:
- 1 cup buckwheat flour
- ½ teaspoon sea salt
- 2 tablespoons coconut oil (1 tablespoon melted)
- 1½ cups almond milk, or water
- 1 egg
- 1 teaspoon vanilla extract
- 3 cups fresh berries, divided
- 6 tablespoons Chia Jam, divided

Directions:
1. Whisk together the buckwheat flour, salt, 1 tablespoon of melted coconut oil, almond milk, egg, and vanilla in a small bowl until smooth.
2. Melt the remaining 1 tablespoon of coconut oil in a large (12-inch) nonstick skillet over medium-high heat. Tilt the pan, coating it evenly with the melted oil.
3. Into the skillet, ladle ¼ cup of batter. Tilt the skillet to coat it evenly with the batter.
4. Cook for 2 minutes, or until the edges begin to curl up. Flip the crêpe and cook for 1 minute on the second side using a spatula. Transfer the crêpe to a plate.
5. Continue to make crêpes with the remaining batter. You should have 4 to 6 crêpes.
6. Place 1 crêpe on a plate, top with ½ cup of berries and 1 tablespoon of Chia Jam. Fold the crêpe over the filling. Repeat with the remaining crêpes and serve.

Nutrition Info:
- Info Per Serving: Calories: 242 ;Fat: 11g ;Protein: 7g ;Carbs: 33g .

Pumpkin Cake With Pistachios

Servings: 4
Cooking Time: 70 Minutes
Ingredients:
- 2 eggs
- 3 tbsp avocado oil
- ¾ cup pumpkin, shredded
- ½ cup pure maple syrup
- 3 tbsp pure date sugar
- 1 ½ cups whole-wheat flour
- ½ tsp cinnamon powder
- ½ tsp baking powder
- ¼ tsp cloves powder
- ½ tsp allspice powder
- ½ tsp nutmeg powder
- 2 tbsp chopped pistachios

Directions:
1. Preheat your oven to 350ºF. Lightly coat a loaf pan with cooking spray. In a bowl, whisk avocado oil, pumpkin, maple syrup, date sugar, and eggs. In another bowl, mix the flour, cinnamon powder, baking powder, cloves powder, allspice powder, and nutmeg powder. Add this mixture to the wet batter and mix until well combined. Pour the batter into the loaf pan, sprinkle the pistachios on top, and gently press the nuts onto the batter to stick.

2. Bake in the oven for 50-55 minutes or until a toothpick inserted into the cake comes out clean. Remove the cake onto a wire rack, allow cooling, slice, and serve.

Nutrition Info:

- Info Per Serving: Calories: 368;Fat: 5g;Protein: 8.8g;Carbs: 73.7g.

Green Banana Smoothie

Servings: 2

Cooking Time: 5 Minutes

Ingredients:

- 2 cups flaxseed milk
- 2 cups spinach, chopped
- 2 bananas, peeled
- 1 packet stevia
- 1 tsp ground cinnamon
- 1 cup crushed ice

Directions:

1. Place the flaxseed milk, spinach, bananas, stevia, cinnamon, and ice in a food processor and pulse until smooth. Serve immediately.

Nutrition Info:

- Info Per Serving: Calories: 180;Fat: 5g;Protein: 4g;Carbs: 38g.

Terrific Pancakes With Coconut And Banana

Servings: 4

Cooking Time: 10 Minutes

Ingredients:

- ½ cup almond flour
- ¼ cup coconut flour
- 1 teaspoon baking soda
- 3 eggs, beaten
- 2 bananas, mashed
- 1 teaspoon pure vanilla extract
- 1 tablespoon coconut oil

Directions:

1. Stir the almond flour, coconut flour, and baking soda together in a medium bowl until well mixed.

2. Make a well in the center and add the eggs, bananas, and vanilla. Beat together until well blended.

3. Place a large skillet over medium-high heat and add the coconut oil.

4. Pour ¼ cup of batter into the skillet, four per batch for each pancake. Cook for about 3 minutes, or until the bottom is golden and the bubbles on the surface burst. Flip and cook for about 2 minutes more until golden and cooked through. Transfer to a plate and repeat with any remaining batter.

5. Serve the pancake.

Nutrition Info:

- Info Per Serving: Calories: 218 ;Fat: 15g ;Protein: 8g;Carbs: 17g .

Hazelnut & Raspberry Quinoa

Servings: 4

Cooking Time: 30 Minutes

Ingredients:

- ½ cup shredded coconut
- 1 cup quinoa, rinsed well
- ¼ cup hemp seeds
- 1 tsp ground cinnamon
- 2 tbsp flaxseeds
- 1 tsp vanilla extract
- Sea salt to taste
- ¼ cup chopped hazelnuts
- 1 cup fresh raspberries

Directions:

1. Boil the quinoa with 2 cups of water in a saucepan over medium heat for 18-20 minutes. Mix in the hemp seeds, coconut, cinnamon, flaxseeds, vanilla, and salt. Serve the quinoa with hazelnuts and raspberries on top.

Nutrition Info:

- Info Per Serving: Calories: 290;Fat: 15g;Protein: 9g;Carbs: 32g.

Poultry And Meats

Grilled Chicken Sandwiches

Servings: 4
Cooking Time: 20 Minutes
Ingredients:

- 2 tbsp olive oil
- 4 chicken breast halves
- Sea salt and pepper to taste
- 6 roasted red pepper slices
- 1 tbsp Dijon mustard
- ¼ cup paleo mayonnaise
- 4 whole-wheat buns, halved

Directions:

1. Pound the chicken with a rolling pin to ½-inch thickness. Preheat your grill to medium-high heat. Sprinkle the chicken breasts with salt and pepper and brush them with olive oil. Place them on the hot grill and cook for 8 minutes on all sides until cooked through.

2. In the meantime, place the mustard, mayonnaise, and 2 red pepper slices in a food processor and pulse until smooth. To make the sandwiches, cover the bottom halves of the buns with the mayo mixture, followed by the remaining roasted pepper slices and chicken. Finish with the top bun halves. Serve immediately.

Nutrition Info:

- Info Per Serving: Calories: 320;Fat: 16g;Protein: 7g;Carbs: 37g.

Broccoli & Chicken Stir-fry

Servings: 4
Cooking Time: 20 Minutes
Ingredients:

- 2 cups broccoli florets
- 1 ½ lb chicken breasts, cubed
- ½ onion, chopped
- Sea salt and pepper to taste
- 3 tbsp extra-virgin olive oil
- 3 garlic cloves, minced

Directions:

1. Warm the olive oil in a skillet over medium heat. Add the broccoli, chicken, garlic, and onion and stir-fry for about 8 minutes, or until the chicken is golden browned and cooked through. Season with salt and pepper. Serve.

Nutrition Info:

- Info Per Serving: Calories: 345;Fat: 13g;Protein: 13g;Carbs: 4g.

Gingered Beef Stir-fry With Peppers

Servings: 4
Cooking Time: 15 Minutes
Ingredients:

- 2 tbsp olive oil
- 1 lb ground beef
- 2 green garlic stalks, minced
- 6 scallions, chopped
- 2 red bell peppers, chopped
- 2 tbsp grated fresh ginger
- ½ tsp sea salt
- 2 tbsp tarragon, chopped

Directions:

1. Warm the olive oil in a skillet over medium heat and place the ground beef. Cook for 5 minutes until browns. Stir in scallions, green garlic, bell peppers, ginger, and salt and cook for 4 more minutes until the bell peppers are soft. Top with tarragon and serve immediately.

Nutrition Info:

- Info Per Serving: Calories: 600;Fat: 20g;Protein: 2g;Carbs: 10g.

Smoky Lamb Souvlaki

Servings: 4
Cooking Time: 25 Minutes + Marinating Time
Ingredients:

- 1 lb lamb shoulder, cubed
- 2 tbsp olive oil
- 1 tbsp apple cider vinegar
- 2 tsp crushed fennel seeds
- 2 tsp smoked paprika
- Salt and garlic powder to taste

Directions:

1. Blend the olive oil, cider vinegar, crushed fennel seeds, smoked paprika, garlic powder, and sea salt in a large bowl. Stir in the lamb. Cover the bowl and refrigerate it for 1 hour to marinate. Preheat a frying pan over high heat. Thread 4-5 pieces of lamb each onto 8 skewers. Fry for 3-4 minutes per side until cooked through. Serve.

Nutrition Info:

- Info Per Serving: Calories: 275;Fat: 15g;Protein: 31g;Carbs: 1g.

Creamy Turkey With Mushrooms

Servings: 4
Cooking Time: 40 Minutes
Ingredients:

- 1 ½ lb turkey breasts, boneless and skinless
- 6 oz white button mushrooms, sliced
- 3 tbsp chopped shallots
- ½ tsp dried thyme
- ½ cup dry white wine
- 1 cup chicken stock
- 1 garlic clove, minced
- 2 tbsp olive oil
- 3 tbsp coconut cream
- 1 ½ tbsp arrowroot
- Sea salt and pepper to taste

Directions:

1. Tie the turkey breast with a kitchen string horizontally, leaving approximately 2 inches apart. Season with salt and pepper. Heat half of the olive oil in your Instant Pot on "Sauté". Add the turkey and brown it for 3 minutes on each side. Transfer to a plate. Add the remaining oil, followed by the shallots, thyme, garlic, and mushrooms and cook for 5 minutes or until translucent. Add white wine and scrape up the brown bits from the bottom.

2. When the alcohol evaporates, return the turkey to the pot. Add the broth. Close the lid and cook for 20 minutes on "Manual". Combine the coconut cream and arrowroot in a bowl. Stir in the pot. Bring the sauce to a boil, then turn the cooker off. Slice the turkey in half and serve topped with the creamy mushroom sauce.

Nutrition Info:

- Info Per Serving: Calories: 192;Fat: 5g;Protein: 15g;Carbs: 12g.

Delightful Stuffed Lamb With Peppers

Servings: 6
Cooking Time: 60 Minutes
Ingredients:

- 1 onion, finely diced
- 2 tablespoons water, plus additional for cooking
- 1½ pounds lamb, ground
- 1 cup grated zucchini
- ¼ cup fresh basil, minced
- 1 teaspoon salt
- 6 bell peppers, any color, seeded, ribbed, tops removed and reserved

Directions:

1. Preheat the oven to 350°F.
2. Sauté the onion in the water in a large pan set over medium heat for 5 minutes, or until soft.
3. Add the ground lamb and zucchini. Cook for 10 minutes by breaking up the meat with a spoon.
4. Stir in the basil and salt. Remove from the heat.
5. Fill a casserole dish with 1½ inches of water.
6. Stuff each pepper with an equal amount of the lamb mixture and place them into the dish. Cap each pepper with its reserved top.
7. Place the dish in the preheated oven and bake for 45 to 50 minutes.

Nutrition Info:

- Info Per Serving: Calories: 258 ;Fat: 9g Protein: 348g ;;Carbs: 10g.

Classic And Minty Lamb Burgers

Servings: 2
Cooking Time: 20 Minutes
Ingredients:

- 8 oz ground lamb, lean
- 1 tablespoon fresh rosemary, finely chopped
- ½ cup extra virgin olive oil
- 1 lemon, juiced
- 1 clove of garlic, minced
- ½ cup of low-fat Greek yogurt
- ¼ cucumber, chopped
- ½ bunch fresh mint
- ½ cup arugula

Directions:

1. Mix together the ground lamb, garlic, and rosemary and a drizzle of the olive oil until combined, and then shape 1-inch-thick patties with your hands.
2. Heat the rest of the oil in a skillet over medium-high heat, and then cook the patties for 16 minutes, flipping once halfway through and ensuring they are cooked throughout.
3. Mix the yogurt, lemon juice, mint, and cucumber and serve on top of the lamb burger with a side salad of arugula.
4. Serve warm.

Nutrition Info:

- Info Per Serving: Calories: 1050 ;Fat: 79g ;Protein: 54g ;Carbs: 31g .

Rosemary Lamb Chops

Servings: 4

Cooking Time: 50 Minutes + Marinating Time

Ingredients:

* 4 garlic cloves, mashed
* 8 lamb chops
* 2 tbsp chopped rosemary
* ¼ cup extra-virgin olive oil
* 1 tsp Dijon mustard
* Sea salt and pepper to taste

Directions:

1. Mix the olive oil, rosemary, garlic, Dijon mustard, salt, and pepper in a bowl. Add the lamb chops and toss to coat R. Cover the dish with plastic wrap and marinate the chops at room temperature for 30 minutes. Preheat your oven to 425ºF. Bake the lamb chops for 15-20 minutes, or until they are sizzling and browned. Serve.

Nutrition Info:

* Info Per Serving: Calories: 645;Fat: 33g;Protein: 79g;Carbs: 3g.

Good For The Bones Stir Fried Sesame Chicken

Servings: 6

Cooking Time: 25 Minutes

Ingredients:

* ¾ cup warm water
* ½ cup tahini
* ¼ cup plus 2 tablespoons toasted sesame oil, divided
* 2 garlic cloves, minced
* ½ teaspoon salt
* 1 pound boneless skinless chicken breasts, cut into ½-inch cubes
* 6 cups lightly packed kale, thoroughly washed and chopped

Directions:

1. Whisk together in a medium bowl the warm water, tahini, ¼ cup of sesame oil, garlic, and salt.
2. Heat the remaining 2 tablespoons of sesame oil in a large pan set over medium heat.
3. Add the chicken and cook for 8 to 10 minutes while stirring.
4. Stir in the tahini-sesame sauce. Mix it well to coat the chicken. Cook for 6 to 8 minutes more.
5. Add the kale one handful at a time. When the first handful wilts, add the next. Continue until all the kale has been added. Serve hot.

Nutrition Info:

* Info Per Serving: Calories: 417 ;Fat: 30g ;Protein: 27g ;Carbs: 12g .

Tomato & Lentil Lamb Ragù

Servings: 4

Cooking Time: 40 Minutes

Ingredients:

* 1 red onion, chopped
* 4 garlic cloves, minced
* 1 lb ground lamb
* 14 oz canned diced tomatoes
* 1 cup chicken broth
* 2 tbsp extra-virgin olive oil
* ½ cup green lentils
* Sea salt and pepper to taste
* 1 tsp ginger powder
* 1 tsp ground cumin

Directions:

1. Warm the olive oil in a large pan over high heat. Add the onion and garlic sauté for 3 minutes. Add the ground lamb, breaking it up with a spoon. Brown for 3-4 minutes. Stir in the tomatoes, chicken broth, lentils, salt, ginger powder, cumin, and pepper. Simmer for 20 minutes, or until the lentils are cooked and most of the liquid has evaporated. Serve and enjoy!

Nutrition Info:

* Info Per Serving: Calories: 400;Fat: 15g;Protein: 40g;Carbs: 23g.

Korean Chicken Thighs

Servings: 4

Cooking Time: 4 Hours 10 Minutes

Ingredients:

* 8 boneless, skinless chicken thighs
* ¼ cup miso paste
* 2 tbsp coconut oil, melted
* 1 tbsp honey
* 1 tbsp rice wine vinegar
* 2 garlic cloves, sliced
* 1 tsp minced ginger root
* 2 red chilies, sliced
* 1 cup chicken broth
* 2 scallions, sliced
* 1 tbsp sesame seeds

Directions:

1. Place the miso, coconut oil, honey, rice wine vinegar, garlic, chilies, and ginger root in your slow cooker and mix well. Add the chicken. Cover and cook on "High" for 4 hours. Top with scallions and sesame seeds. Serve.

- Info Per Serving: Calories: 315;Fat: 14g;Protein: 31g;Carbs: 17g.

Port Wine Garlicky Lamb

Servings: 4

Cooking Time: 30 Minutes

Ingredients:

- 2 lb lamb shanks
- 1 tbsp olive oil
- ½ cup Port wine
- 1 tbsp tomato paste
- 10 peeled whole garlic cloves
- ½ cup chicken broth
- 1 tsp balsamic vinegar
- ½ tsp dried rosemary
- 1 tbsp olive oil

Directions:

1. Heat the oil in the Instant Pot on "Sauté" and brown the lamb shanks on all sides. Add the garlic and cook until lightly browned, no more than 2 minutes. Stir in the rest of the ingredients, except the oil and vinegar. Seal the lid and cook for 20 minutes on "Manual" on high. When cooking is complete, release the pressure naturally for 10 minutes. Remove the lamb shanks and let the sauce boil for 5 minutes with the lid off. Stir in the vinegar and butter. Serve the gravy poured over the shanks.

Nutrition Info:

- Info Per Serving: Calories: 620;Fat: 35g;Protein: 60g;Carbs: 9g.

Marvellous Chocolate Chili

Servings: 4 To 6

Cooking Time: 45 Minutes

Ingredients:

- 1 tablespoon extra-virgin olive oil
- 1 pound lean ground beef
- 1 large onion, chopped
- 2 garlic cloves, minced
- 1 tablespoon cocoa, unsweetened
- 1½ teaspoons chili powder
- 1 teaspoon salt
- ½ teaspoon cumin, ground
- 2 cups chicken broth
- 1 cup tomato sauce

Directions:

1. Heat the oil over high heat in a Dutch oven. Add the ground beef and brown well for 5 minutes.

2. Add the onion, garlic, cocoa, chili powder, salt, and cumin and cook while stirring for a minute.

3. Add the chicken broth and tomato sauce and bring to a boil. Reduce the heat to a simmer, cover, and cook, stirring occasionally for 30 to 40 minutes. Add more chicken broth or water if the sauce becomes too thick as it cooks to thin it.

4. Ladle into bowls and serve.

Nutrition Info:

- Info Per Serving: Calories: 370 ;Fat: 27g ;Protein: 23g ;Carbs: 9g.

Mustardy Beef Steaks

Servings: 4

Cooking Time: 60 Minutes

Ingredients:

- ½ cup olive oil
- 2 tbsp Dijon mustard
- ½ cup balsamic vinegar
- 2 garlic cloves, minced
- 1 tsp rosemary, chopped
- 4 (½-inch thick) beef steaks
- Sea salt and pepper to taste

Directions:

1. Combine the olive oil, mustard, vinegar, garlic, rosemary, salt, and pepper in a bowl. Add in steaks and toss to coat. Let marinate covered for 30 minutes. Remove any excess of the marinade from the steaks and transfer them to a warm skillet over high heat and cook for 4-6 minutes on both sides. Let sit for 5 minutes and serve.

Nutrition Info:

- Info Per Serving: Calories: 480;Fat: 3g;Protein: 48g;Carbs: 4g.

Homemade Pizza With Lean Meat, Jalapeno, And Tapioca Starch

Servings: 4

Cooking Time: 40 Minutes

Ingredients:

- Base:
- 1 cup tapioca starch
- ½ cup coconut flour
- 2 free-range eggs
- 1 cup water
- Topping:
- ½ can chopped tomatoes
- 1 clove garlic, minced
- 1 sprig rosemary
- 1 sprig basil

- 2 beef tomatoes, sliced
- 1 jalapeno, sliced
- ½ cup watercress or spinach
- 1 onion, chopped
- ½ cup lean meat, cooked and sliced

Directions:

1. Heat oven to 375°F.

2. In a bowl, mix together all of the ingredients for the base until a smooth dough is formed. Add a little more water if necessary.

3. Roll the dough into a pizza base.

4. Sauté onions and garlic over medium heat and add chopped tomatoes and herbs then cook for 5 to 10 minutes.

5. On a slatted rack, layer the base with the tomato sauce, jalapeno, herbs, tomato slices, and meat pieces, and then bake in the oven for 30 minutes.

6. Ensure the base is cooked through and not soggy.

7. Cut into eights then serve immediately with the watercress or spinach scattered on top.

Nutrition Info:

- Info Per Serving: Calories: 227 ;Fat: 1g ;Protein: 13g ;Carbs: 40g .

Incredible Tacos With Pork

Servings: 4 To 6
Cooking Time: 7 To 8 Hours
Ingredients:

- 1 teaspoon sea salt
- 1 teaspoon cumin, ground
- 1 teaspoon garlic powder
- ½ teaspoon oregano, dried
- ½ teaspoon black pepper, freshly ground
- 3 to 4 pounds pork shoulder or butt
- 2 cups broth of choice
- Juice of 1 orange
- 1 small onion, chopped
- 4 to 6 corn taco shells
- Shredded cabbage, lime wedges, avocado, and hot sauce

Directions:

1. Stir together in a small bowl the salt, cumin, garlic powder, oregano, and pepper. Rub the pork with the spice mixture and put it in your slow cooker.

2. Pour the broth and orange juice around the pork. Scatter the onion around the pork.

3. Cover the cooker and set on low. Cook for 7 to 8 hours.

4. Transfer the pork to a work surface and shred it with a fork. Serve in taco shells with any optional toppings you like.

Nutrition Info:

- Info Per Serving: Calories: 1156 ;Fat: 84g ;Protein: 84g ;Carbs: 12g .

Veggie & Beef Brisket

Servings: 4
Cooking Time: 60 Minutes
Ingredients:

- 4 beef tenderloin fillets
- 4 sweet potatoes, chopped
- 1 onion, chopped
- 2 bay leaves
- 2 tbsp olive oil
- 2 cups chopped carrots
- 3 tbsp chopped garlic
- 3 tbsp Worcestershire sauce
- 2 celery stalks, chopped
- Black pepper to taste
- 1 tbsp Knorr demi-glace sauce

Directions:

1. Heat 1 tbsp oil in your pressure cooker on "Sauté". Sauté the onion until caramelized. Transfer to a bowl. Season the meat with pepper to taste. Heat the remaining oil and cook the meat until browned on all sides. Add the remaining ingredients and 2 cups of water. Close the lid and cook for 30 minutes on "Manual" on High pressure. When cooking is complete, release the pressure naturally for 10 minutes. Transfer the meat and veggies to a serving platter. Whisk the Knorr Demi-Glace sauce in the pot and simmer for 5 minutes until thickened on "Sauté". Pour the gravy over the meat and enjoy.

Nutrition Info:

- Info Per Serving: Calories: 400;Fat: 20g;Protein: 28g;Carbs: 10g.

Grilled Beef Burgers With Chipotle Aioli

Servings: 4
Cooking Time: 20 Minutes
Ingredients:

- 1 tbsp olive oil
- 4 beef burgers
- ½ cup chipotle aioli
- 4 tsp low-sodium soy sauce
- 2 tbsp brown sugar
- 2 tbsp chopped scallions

Directions:

1. Preheat your grill to medium-high heat. Cook the burgers on the grill to the desired doneness, about 10

minutes. Combine the aioli, soy sauce, brown sugar, and scallions in a bowl. Top each burger with the sauce and serve.

Nutrition Info:

- Info Per Serving: Calories: 340;Fat: 19g;Protein: 1g;Carbs: 14g.

Worth It Glazed Chicken Thighs With Cauliflower

Servings: 4

Cooking Time: 35 To 40 Minutes

Ingredients:

- ½ cup balsamic vinegar
- ¼ cup extra-virgin olive oil
- 2 tablespoons maple syrup
- 8 bone-in chicken thighs, 2 to 3 ounces
- 2 cauliflower heads, broken or cut into florets
- Salt

Directions:

1. Whisk together the balsamic vinegar, olive oil, and maple syrup in a small bowl.
2. Combine in a medium dish the chicken thighs and vinegar-maple mixture. Marinate the chicken for 30 minutes in the refrigerator.
3. Preheat the oven to 350°F.
4. Cover the chicken with aluminum foil and place it in the preheated oven. Bake for 30 to 35 minutes, or until the chicken is cooked through. The internal temperature should be 165°F.
5. Leave the chicken in the oven uncovered if you've left the skin on the chicken for 10 minutes more to crisp the skin.
6. Fill a large pot with 2 inches of water and insert a steamer basket. Bring to a boil over high heat. Add the cauliflower then cover and steam for 8 minutes.
7. Serve the chicken with the cauliflower. Drizzle the extra marinade from the casserole dish over the cauliflower, and season with salt, if necessary.

Nutrition Info:

- Info Per Serving: Calories: 535 ;Fat: 38g ;Protein: 33g ;Carbs: 14g .

Tangy Beef Ribs

Servings: 4

Cooking Time: 2 Hours 10 Minutes

Ingredients:

- 1 cup red wine
- 1 ½ lb beef short ribs
- 1 tsp mustard powder
- ½ tsp garlic powder

- Sea salt and pepper to taste
- 2 tbsp olive oil
- 2 cups beef broth
- 4 sprigs rosemary

Directions:

1. Preheat your oven to 350ºF. Rub the short ribs with mustard powder, garlic powder, salt, and black pepper. Let stand for 10 minutes. Warm the olive oil in a skillet over medium heat. Add the short ribs and sear for 5 minutes or until well browned. Flip the ribs halfway through. Transfer the ribs onto a plate and set aside.
2. Pour the beef broth and red wine into the skillet. Stir to combine well and bring to a boil. Turn down the heat to low and simmer for 10 minutes until the mixture reduces to two-thirds. Put the ribs back to the skillet. Add the rosemary sprigs. Put the skillet lid on, then braise in the oven for 2 hours until the ribs are browned and sticky. Discard the rosemary sprigs. Pour the cooking liquid over and serve warm.

Nutrition Info:

- Info Per Serving: Calories: 730;Fat: 70g;Protein: 24g;Carbs: 2g.

Cumin Lamb Meatballs With Aioli

Servings: 4

Cooking Time: 30 Minutes

Ingredients:

- 1 tsp ground cumin
- 2 tbsp chopped cilantro
- 1 ½ lb ground lamb
- 1 tbsp dried oregano
- 1 tsp onion powder
- 1 tsp garlic powder
- Sea salt and pepper to taste
- ½ cup garlic aioli

Directions:

1. Preheat your oven to 400°F. Combine the ground lamb, cumin, cilantro, rosemary, oregano, onion powder, garlic powder, salt, and pepper in a bowl. Shape 20 meatballs out of the mixture and transfer to a parchment-lined baking sheet. Bake for 15 minutes until the meat reaches an internal temperature of 140°F. Serve warm with aioli.

Nutrition Info:

- Info Per Serving: Calories: 450;Fat: 24g;Protein: 2g;Carbs: 11g.

Italian Turkey Meatballs

Servings: 4

Cooking Time: 7 Hours 15 Minutes

Ingredients:

- 1 spaghetti squash, halved lengthwise, scoop out seeds
- 1 can diced tomatoes
- ½ tsp garlic powder
- ½ tsp dried oregano
- ½ tsp sea salt
- 1 large egg, whisked
- ½ white onion, minced
- 1 lb ground turkey
- Sea salt and pepper to taste
- ½ tsp dried basil
- 1 cup arugula

Directions:

1. Pour the diced tomatoes into your slow cooker. Sprinkle with garlic powder, oregano, and salt. Put in the squash halves, cut-side down. In a medium bowl, mix together the turkey, egg, onion, salt, pepper, and basil. Shape the turkey mixture into balls and place them in the slow cooker around the spaghetti squash. Cover the cooker and set to "Low". Cook for 7 hours. Transfer the squash to a work surface and use a fork to shred it into spaghetti-like strands. Combine the strands with the tomato sauce, top with the meatballs and arugula, and serve.

Nutrition Info:

- Info Per Serving: Calories: 250;Fat: 8g;Protein: 23g;Carbs: 21g.

Tastylicious Chicken Cajun With Prawn

Servings: 2

Cooking Time: 35 Minutes

Ingredients:

- 2 free range chicken breasts, chopped and skinless
- 1 onion, chopped
- 1 red pepper, chopped
- 2 garlic cloves, crushed
- 10 king prawns, fresh or frozen
- 1 teaspoon cayenne pepper
- 1 teaspoon chili powder
- 1 teaspoon paprika
- ¼ teaspoon chili powder
- 1 teaspoon oregano, dried
- 1 teaspoon thyme, dried
- 1 cup rice, brown or wholegrain
- 1 tablespoon extra-virgin olive oil
- 1 can tomatoes, chopped
- 2 cups homemade chicken stock

Directions:

1. Mix the spices and herbs in a separate bowl to form your Cajun spice mix.

2. Grab a large pan and add the olive oil, heating on medium heat.

3. Add the chicken and brown each side for around 4 to 5 minutes then place to one side.

4. Add the onion to the pan and fry until soft.

5. Add the garlic, prawns, Cajun seasoning, and red pepper to the pan and cook for 5 minutes or until prawns become opaque.

6. Add the brown rice along with the chopped tomatoes, chicken, and chicken stock to the pan.

7. Cover the pan and allow to simmer for 25 minutes or until the rice is soft.

Nutrition Info:

- Info Per Serving: Calories: 173 ;Fat: 7g ;Protein: 8g ;Carbs: 21g .

Fiery Pork Loin With Lime

Servings: 4 To 6

Cooking Time: 6 To 7 Hours

Ingredients:

- 3 teaspoons chili powder
- 2 teaspoons garlic powder
- 1 teaspoon cumin, ground
- ½ teaspoon sea salt
- 2 pork tenderloins, 1-pound
- 1 cup broth of choice
- ¼ cup lime juice, freshly squeezed

Directions:

1. Stir together in a small bowl the chili powder, garlic powder, cumin, and salt. Rub the pork all over with the spice mixture and put it in the slow cooker.

2. Pour the broth and lime juice around the pork in the cooker.

3. Cover the cooker and set to low. Cook for 6 to 7 hours.

4. Remove the pork from the slow cooker and let rest for 5 minutes. Before serving, slice the pork against the grain into medallions.

Nutrition Info:

- Info Per Serving: Calories: 259 ;Fat: 5g ;Protein: 50g ;Carbs: 5g .

Paleo Turkey Thighs With Mushroom

Servings: 4

Cooking Time: 4 Hours

Ingredients:

- 1 tablespoon extra-virgin olive oil
- 2 turkey thighs
- 2 cups button or cremini mushrooms, sliced
- 1 large onion, sliced
- 1 garlic clove, sliced
- 1 rosemary sprig
- 1 teaspoon salt
- ¼ teaspoon black pepper, freshly ground
- 2 cups chicken broth
- ½ cup dry red wine

Directions:

1. Into a slow cooker, drizzle the olive oil. Add the turkey thighs, mushrooms, onion, garlic, rosemary sprig, salt, and pepper. Pour in the chicken broth and wine. Cover and cook on high for 4 hours.

2. Remove and discard the rosemary sprig. Transfer the thighs to a plate using a slotted spoon and allow them to cool for several minutes for easier handling.

3. Cut the meat from the bones, stir the meat into the mushrooms, and serve.

Nutrition Info:

- Info Per Serving: Calories: 280 ;Fat: 9g ;Protein: 43g ;Carbs: 3g .

Italian Spinach Chicken

Servings: 4

Cooking Time: 15 Minutes

Ingredients:

- 1 cup chopped spinach
- 2 lb chicken breasts, halved
- ½ cup chicken broth
- 2 garlic cloves, minced
- 2 tbsp olive oil
- ¾ cup heavy cream
- ½ cup sun-dried tomatoes
- 2 tsp Italian seasoning
- ½ cup Parmesan, grated
- ½ tsp sea salt

Directions:

1. Rub the meat with oil, garlic, salt, and seasonings. Add the chicken in your Instant Pot, select "Sauté" and brown it on all sides. Pour the broth in, seal the lid and cook for 5 minutes on "Manual" on high pressure. When it is done,

release the pressure quickly, open the lid and add the cream. Simmer for 5 minutes with the lid off, then stir in the Parmesan cheese. Stir in tomatoes and spinach and cook on "Sauté" just until the spinach wilts. Serve.

Nutrition Info:

- Info Per Serving: Calories: 460;Fat: 25g;Protein: 57g;Carbs: 3g.

Awesome Herbaceous Roasted Chuck And Scrummy Vegetable

Servings: 4

Cooking Time: 7 Hours

Ingredients:

- 16 ounces chuck roast, lean
- 1 teaspoon pepper
- 2 onions cut, peeled and quartered
- 8 baby carrots, peeled and quartered
- 1 stalk of celery, sliced
- 1 bay leaf
- 10 cups water
- 1 cauliflower, cut into florets
- 5 cherry tomatoes
- Seasoning:
- 1 tablespoon cayenne pepper
- 2 tablespoons rosemary, dried or fresh

Directions:

1. Use a sharp knife to trim any fat from the chuck roast.

2. Season with herbs and spices.

3. Put the onions, carrots, and celery into the crockpot or slow cooker, then the meat, and finally add the bay leaf and water.

4. Cook on low for 5 to 7 hours or until the meat is tender.

5. You can add the cauliflower and cherry tomatoes for the last 15 minutes or until cooked through.

6. Serve hot.

Nutrition Info:

- Info Per Serving: Calories: 170 ;Fat: 5g ;Protein: 22g ;Carbs: 10g.

Chicken Satay

Servings: 4

Cooking Time: 25 Minutes + Marinating Time

Ingredients:

- 1 garlic clove, minced
- ½ cup peanut butter
- 2 tbsp coconut aminos
- 1 tbsp grated fresh ginger
- 3 tbsp lime juice

- 1 tsp raw honey
- 2 tsp sriracha sauce
- 1 ½ lb chicken breasts, cut into strips
- 2 tbsp olive oil
- 1 tbsp chopped cilantro

Directions:

1. Combine the peanut butter, ¼ cup of water, coconut aminos, ginger, 1 tbsp of lime juice, garlic, and honey in your food processor and pulse until smooth. Set aside the sauce. In a large bowl, whisk the remaining lime juice, cilantro, and sriracha sauce. Add the chicken strips and toss to coat. Cover the bowl with plastic wrap and refrigerate for 1 hour to marinate.

2. Preheat your oven to broil. Thread each chicken strip onto a wooden skewer and lay them on a rimmed baking sheet. Broil the chicken for about 4 minutes per side until cooked through and golden, turning once. Serve with previously prepared sauce.

Nutrition Info:

- Info Per Serving: Calories: 500;Fat: 28g;Protein: 45g;Carbs: 15g.

Traditional Beef Bolognese

Servings: 4

Cooking Time: 8 Hours 15 Minutes

Ingredients:

- 3 garlic cloves, minced
- 1 tbsp extra-virgin olive oil
- 1 chopped onion
- 1 chopped celery stalk
- 1 chopped carrot
- 1 lb ground beef
- 1 can diced tomatoes
- 1 tbsp white wine vinegar
- ⅛ tsp ground nutmeg
- ½ cup red wine
- ½ tsp red pepper flakes
- Sea salt and pepper to taste

Directions:

1. Grease your slow cooker with olive oil. Add onion, garlic, celery, carrot, ground beef, tomatoes, vinegar, nutmeg, wine, pepper flakes, salt, and pepper. Using a fork, break up the ground beef as much as possible. Cover the cooker and cook for 8 hours on "Low". Serve and enjoy!

Nutrition Info:

- Info Per Serving: Calories: 315;Fat: 20g;Protein: 21g;Carbs: 10g.

Nut Free Turkey Burgers With Ginger

Servings: 4

Cooking Time: 10 Minutes

Ingredients:

- 1½ pounds turkey, ground
- 1 large egg, lightly beaten
- 2 tablespoons coconut flour
- ½ cup onion, finely chopped
- 1 garlic clove, minced
- 2 teaspoons fresh ginger root, minced
- 1 tablespoon cilantro, fresh
- 1 teaspoon salt
- ¼ teaspoon black pepper, freshly ground
- 1 tablespoon extra-virgin olive oil

Directions:

1. Combine in a medium bowl the ground turkey, egg, flour, onion, garlic, ginger root, cilantro, salt, and pepper and mix well.

2. Form the turkey mixture into four patties.

3. Heat the olive oil in a large skillet over medium-high heat.

4. Cook the burgers and flip it once until firm for 3 to 4 minutes on each side. Serve.

Nutrition Info:

- Info Per Serving: Calories: 320 ;Fat: 20g ;Protein: 34g ;Carbs: 2g .

Fish And Seafood

Sheet Pan Baked Salmon With Asparagus

Servings: 4
Cooking Time: 20 Minutes
Ingredients:

- 1 red bell pepper, sliced
- 1 lb asparagus, trimmed
- 2 tbsp olive oil
- Sea salt and pepper to taste
- 4 salmon fillets
- 1 lemon, zested and sliced

Directions:

1. Preheat your oven to 425°F. Season the asparagus and red pepper slices with salt and drizzle with olive oil. Arrange them on a sheet pan. Sprinkle salmon fillets with pepper and salt and put them skin-side down on top of the vegetables. Garnish with lemon zest and lemon slices. Place in the oven and roast for 12-15 minutes until the salmon is cooked through. Serve warm.

Nutrition Info:

- Info Per Serving: Calories: 310;Fat: 19g;Protein: 3g;Carbs: 6g.

Avocado & Tuna Toast

Servings: 4
Cooking Time: 15 Minutes
Ingredients:

- 2 cans wild-caught albacore tuna
- 1 shallot, minced
- 4 sourdough bread slices
- ¼ cup paleo mayonnaise
- 1 tsp lemon juice
- ¼ tsp paprika
- 1 avocado, cut into 8 slices
- 1 tomato, cut into 8 slices
- 3 tsp grated Parmesan cheese

Directions:

1. Preheat your broiler to high. Line a baking sheet with foil. Place the bread slices on the sheet. Combine the mayonnaise, tuna, lemon juice, shallot, and paprika in a bowl and put it on top of each slice. Add in 2 tomato slices and 2 avocado slices on each bread and scatter with 1 tbsp of Parmesan cheese. Place the sheet in the broil and cook for 3-4 minutes. Serve immediately.

Nutrition Info:

- Info Per Serving: Calories: 470;Fat: 28g;Protein: 27g;Carbs: 30g.

Baked Tilapia With Chili Kale

Servings: 2
Cooking Time: 20 Minutes
Ingredients:

- ½ cup whole-grain breadcrumbs
- ½ cup ground hazelnuts
- 2 tilapia fillets, skinless
- 2 tsp extra-virgin olive oil
- 2 tsp whole-grain mustard
- 5 oz kale, chopped
- 1 red chili, sliced
- 1 clove garlic, mashed

Directions:

1. Preheat your oven to 350ºF. Combine the hazelnuts and breadcrumbs in a bowl. Spread a thin layer of mustard over the fish and then dip into the breadcrumb mixture. Transfer to a greased baking dish. Bake for 12 minutes or until cooked through. Warm the olive oil in a skillet over medium heat and sauté the garlic for 30 seconds. Add the kale and red chili and cook for 5 more minutes. Serve fish with the kale on the side.

Nutrition Info:

- Info Per Serving: Calories: 540;Fat: 32g;Protein: 35g;Carbs: 29g.

Lime-avocado Ahi Poke

Servings: 4
Cooking Time: 10 Minutes + Marinating Time
Ingredients:

- 1 lb sushi-grade ahi tuna, cubed
- 1 cucumber, sliced
- 1 large avocado, diced
- 3 tbsp coconut aminos
- 3 scallions, thinly sliced
- 1 serrano chile, minced
- 1 tsp olive oil
- 1 tsp lime juice
- 1 tsp toasted sesame seeds
- ¼ tsp ground ginger

Directions:

1. Mix the ahi tuna cubes with the coconut aminos, scallions, serrano chile, olive oil, lime juice, sesame seeds, and ginger in a large bowl. Cover the bowl with plastic wrap

and marinate in the fridge for 15 minutes. Add the diced avocado to the bowl of ahi poke and stir to incorporate. Arrange the cucumber rounds on a serving plate. Spoon the ahi poke over the cucumber and serve.

Nutrition Info:

- Info Per Serving: Calories: 210;Fat: 15g;Protein: 9g;Carbs: 10g.

Gingery Sea Bass

Servings: 2

Cooking Time: 15 Minutes

Ingredients:

- 2 spring onions, sliced
- 2 sea bass fillets
- 1 tsp black pepper
- 1 tbsp extra-virgin olive oil
- 1 tsp grated ginger
- 1 garlic clove, thinly sliced
- 1 red chili, thinly sliced
- 1 lime, zested

Directions:

1. Warm the olive oil in a skillet over medium heat. Sprinkle black pepper over the fish and score the skin of the fish a few times with a sharp knife. Add the sea bass fillet to the skillet with the skin side down. Cook for 5 minutes and turn over. Cook for a further 2 minutes; reserve.

2. Add the chili, garlic, and ginger to the same skillet and cook for 2 minutes or until golden. Remove from the heat and add the spring onions. Scatter the vegetables and lime zest over your sea bass and serve.

Nutrition Info:

- Info Per Serving: Calories: 205;Fat: 10g;Protein: 24g;Carbs: 5g.

Persian Saucy Sole

Servings: 4

Cooking Time: 40 Minutes

Ingredients:

- 1 red onion, chopped
- 2 tsp minced garlic
- 1 tsp grated fresh ginger
- ¼ tsp turmeric
- 2 lb sole fillets
- Sea salt to taste
- 2 tbsp lemon juice
- 1 tbsp coconut oil
- 1 cup canned coconut milk
- 2 tbsp chopped cilantro

Directions:

1. Preheat your oven to 350ºF. Place the fillets in a baking dish. Sprinkle it with salt and lemon juice. Roast the fish for 10 minutes. Warm the coconut oil in a pan over medium heat. Add the red onion, garlic, and ginger and sauté for about 3 minutes, or until softened.

2. Stir in coconut milk and turmeric. Bring to a boil. Reduce the heat to low and simmer the sauce for 5 minutes. Remove the skillet from the heat. Pour the sauce over the fish. Cover and bake for about 10 minutes, or until the fish flakes easily with a fork. Top with cilantro and serve.

Nutrition Info:

- Info Per Serving: Calories: 350;Fat: 20g;Protein: 29g;Carbs: 6g.

Cool Salmon Burger With Wasabi

Servings: 1

Cooking Time: 10 Minutes

Ingredients:

- ½ teaspoon honey
- 2 tablespoons reduced-salt soy sauce
- 1 teaspoon wasabi powder
- 1 free range egg, beaten
- 2 cans of wild salmon, drained
- 2 scallions, chopped
- 2 tablespoons coconut oil
- 1 tablespoon fresh ginger, minced

Directions:

1. In a bowl, combine the salmon, egg, ginger, scallions and 1 tablespoon oil. Mix it well with your hands to form 4 patties.

2. Add the wasabi powder and soy sauce in a separate bowl with the honey then whisk until it blends.

3. In a skillet, heat 1 tablespoon oil over a medium heat and cook the patties for 4 minutes each side until firm and browned.

4. Glaze the top of each patty with the wasabi mixture and cook for 15 seconds more before you serve.

5. Serve with your favorite side salad or vegetables for a healthy treat.

Nutrition Info:

- Info Per Serving: Calories: 1758 ;Fat: 103g ;Protein: 184g Carbs: 15g .

Creamy Crabmeat

Servings: 4

Cooking Time: 15 Minutes

Ingredients:

- ¼ cup olive oil
- 1 small red onion, chopped
- 1 lb lump crabmeat
- ½ celery stalk, chopped
- ½ cup plain yogurt
- ¼ cup chicken broth

Directions:

1. Season the crabmeat with some salt and pepper. Heat the oil in your Instant Pot on "Sauté". Add celery and onion and cook for 3 minutes, or until soft. Add the crabmeat and stir in the broth. Seal and lock the lid and set to "Steam" for 5 minutes on high pressure. Once the cooking is complete, do a quick release and carefully open the lid. Stir in the yogurt and serve.

Nutrition Info:

- Info Per Serving: Calories: 450;Fat: 10g;Protein: 40g;Carbs: 12g.

Chipotle Trout With Spinach

Servings: 4

Cooking Time: 25 Minutes

Ingredients:

- 2 tbsp olive oil
- 10 oz spinach
- ½ red onion, sliced
- 4 trout fillets, boneless
- 2 tbsp lemon juice
- ¼ tsp garlic powder
- ¼ tsp chipotle powder
- 1 tsp sea salt

Directions:

1. Preheat your oven to 375°F. Grease a baking pan with olive oil and place the spinach and red onion on the bottom. Add in trout fillets, chipotle powder, garlic, and salt and bake covered with foil for 15 minutes. Sprinkle with lemon juice and serve.

Nutrition Info:

- Info Per Serving: Calories: 162;Fat: 8g;Protein: 19g;Carbs: 6g.

Spicy Shrimp Scampi

Servings: 4

Cooking Time: 25 Minutes

Ingredients:

- 1 ½ lb shrimp, peeled and tails removed

- 1 tsp ancho chili powder
- ¼ cup coconut oil
- 1 tsp paprika
- 1 onion, finely chopped
- 1 red bell pepper, chopped
- 2 garlic cloves, minced
- 1 lemon, zested and juiced
- Sea salt and pepper to taste

Directions:

1. Warm the coconut oil in a skillet over medium heat. Add the onion and red bell pepper and cook for 6 minutes until tender. Put in shrimp and cook for 5 minutes until it´s pink. Mix in garlic and cook for another 30 seconds. Add lemon juice, lemon zest, ancho chili powder, paprika, salt, and pepper and simmer for 3 minutes. Serve warm.

Nutrition Info:

- Info Per Serving: Calories: 350;Fat: 17g;Protein: 1g;Carbs: 11g.

Beneficial Baked Salmon Patties With Vegetables

Servings: 4

Cooking Time: 35 To 38 Minutes

Ingredients:

- 2 cups cooked, mashed sweet potatoes (2 large sweet potatoes)
- Two 6 ounces cans wild salmon, drained
- ¼ cup almond flour
- ¼ teaspoon turmeric, ground
- 2 tablespoons coconut oil
- 2 kale bunches, thoroughly washed, stemmed, and cut into ribbons
- ¼ teaspoon salt

Directions:

1. Preheat the oven to 350°F.
2. Line a baking sheet with parchment paper.
3. Stir together the mashed sweet potatoes and salmon in a large bowl.
4. Blend in the almond flour and turmeric.
5. Scoop the salmon mixture onto the baking sheet using a �?cup measure. Flatten slightly with the bottom of the measuring cup. Repeat with the remaining mixture.
6. Place the sheet in the preheated oven and bake for 30 minutes, flipping the patties halfway through.
7. Heat the coconut oil in a large pan set over medium heat.
8. Add the kale. Sauté for 5 to 8 minutes, or until the kale is bright and wilted. Sprinkle with the salt and serve with the salmon patties.

Nutrition Info:

- Info Per Serving: Calories: 320 ;Fat: 13g ;Protein: 21g ;Carbs: 32g .

Lemon Sauce Salmon

Servings: 4

Cooking Time: 20 Minutes

Ingredients:

- 4 salmon fillets
- 1 tbsp honey
- ½ tsp cumin
- 1 tbsp hot water
- 1 tbsp olive oil
- 1 tsp smoked paprika
- 1 tbsp chopped parsley
- ¼ cup lemon juice

Directions:

1. Pour 1 cup of water into the Instant pot, then put the steamer rack in place. Place the salmon on the steamer rack skin side down. Seal the lid and cook for 3 minutes on "Manual". In a bowl, whisk together the remaining ingredients. Once the cooking is over, release the pressure quickly, and drizzle the sauce over the salmon. Seal the lid again and cook for 2 more minutes on "Manual". Then, perform a quick pressure release and serve immediately.

Nutrition Info:

- Info Per Serving: Calories: 495;Fat: 32g;Protein: 41g;Carbs: 6g.

Salmon In Miso-ginger Sauce

Servings: 4

Cooking Time: 30 Minutes

Ingredients:

- 1 sliced scallion
- 4 boneless salmon fillets
- ⅛ tsp red pepper flakes
- 1 tbsp olive oil
- ¼ cup apple cider
- ¼ tsp porcini powder
- ¼ tsp garlic powder
- ¼ cup white miso
- 1 tbsp white rice vinegar
- ⅛ tsp ground ginger

Directions:

1. Whisk olive oil, apple cider, porcini powder, garlic powder, miso, vinegar, and ginger in a bowl. Set aside.

2. Preheat your oven to 375°F. Arrange the salmon fillets, skin-side down on a greased baking pan. Pour the prepared sauce over the fillets. Bake in the oven for 15-20 minutes, or

until the fish flakes easily with a fork. Garnish with scallion and red pepper flakes and serve.

Nutrition Info:

- Info Per Serving: Calories: 465;Fat: 19g;Protein: 67g;Carbs: 9g.

Remarkable Sautéed Sardines With Mash Cauliflower

Servings: 4

Cooking Time: 15 Minutes

Ingredients:

- 2 heads cauliflower, broken into large florets
- 4 tablespoons extra-virgin olive oil, divided
- ¼ teaspoon salt
- Four 4 ounces cans sardines packed in water, drained
- 1 cup fresh parsley, finely chopped

Directions:

1. Fill a large pot with 2 inches of water and insert a steamer basket. Bring the water to a boil over high heat.

2. Add the cauliflower to the basket. For 8 to 10 minutes, cover and steam until the florets are tender. Transfer the cauliflower to a food processor.

3. Add 2 tablespoons of olive oil and salt to the cauliflower. Process until the cauliflower is smooth and creamy. You may need to do this in two batches.

4. Roughly mash the sardines in a medium bowl.

5. Add the remaining 2 tablespoons of olive oil to a medium pan set over low heat. Add the sardines and parsley when oil is shimmering. Cook for 3 minutes. The sardines must be warm, not scalding hot.

6. Serve the sardines with a generous scoop of cauliflower mash.

Nutrition Info:

- Info Per Serving: Calories: 334 ;Fat: 24g ;Protein: 26g ;Carbs: 8g ;Sugar: 3g .

Baked Cod Fillets With Mushroom

Servings: 4

Cooking Time: 30 Minutes

Ingredients:

- 8 oz shiitake mushrooms, sliced
- 1 ½ lb cod fillets
- 1 leek, sliced thin
- Sea salt and pepper to taste
- 1 lemon, zested
- 2 tbsp extra-virgin olive oil
- 1 tbsp coconut aminos
- 1 tsp sweet paprika

½ cup vegetable broth

Directions:

1. Preheat your oven to 375ºF. In a baking dish, combine the olive oil, leek, mushrooms, coconut aminos, lemon zest, paprika, and salt. Place the cod fillets over and sprinkle it with salt and pepper. Pour in the vegetable broth. Bake for 15-20 minutes, or until the cod is firm but cooked through. Serve and enjoy!

Nutrition Info:

- Info Per Serving: Calories: 220;Fat: 5g;Protein: 32g;Carbs: 12g.

Crispy Coconut Prawns

Servings: 2

Cooking Time: 25 Minutes

Ingredients:

- 1 lb prawns, peeled and deveined
- ¼ cup coconut flour
- ½ tsp cayenne pepper
- 1 tsp garlic powder
- 2 beaten eggs
- ½ cup shredded coconut
- ¼ cup almond flour
- Black pepper to taste

Directions:

1. Preheat your oven to 400ºF. Blend the coconut flour, cayenne pepper, and garlic powder in a bowl. In a separate bowl, whisk the eggs. In a third bowl, add the shredded coconut, almond flour and black pepper. Dip the prawns into each dish in consecutive order, and then place a parchment-lined baking sheet. Bake for 10-15 minutes or until cooked through. Serve and enjoy!

Nutrition Info:

- Info Per Serving: Calories: 475;Fat: 15g;Protein: 54g;Carbs: 30g.

Rich Grandma's Salmon Chowder

Servings: 4

Cooking Time: 25 Minutes

Ingredients:

- 2 cans diced tomatoes, 1 drained and 1 undrained
- 2 tbsp fresh chives, chopped
- ¼ cup olive oil
- 1 red bell pepper, chopped
- 1 lb skinless salmon, cubed
- 4 cups fish stock
- 2 cups diced sweet potatoes
- 1 tsp onion powder
- Sea salt and pepper to taste

Directions:

1. Warm the olive oil in a pot over medium heat and place the red bell pepper and salmon. Cook for 5 minutes until the salmon is opaque and the bell pepper is tender. Mix in tomatoes, fish stock, sweet potatoes, onion powder, salt, and pepper and bring to a simmer. Then low the heat and cook for 10 minutes until the potatoes are soft. Divide the chowder between bowls and scatter over the chopped chives. Serve immediately.

Nutrition Info:

- Info Per Serving: Calories: 580;Fat: 43g;Protein: 17g;Carbs: 56g.

Aromatic Curried Whitefish

Servings: 4 To 6

Cooking Time: 15 Minutes

Ingredients:

- 2 tablespoons coconut oil
- 1 onion, chopped
- 2 garlic cloves, minced
- 1 tablespoon fresh ginger, minced
- 2 teaspoons curry powder
- 1 teaspoon salt
- ¼ teaspoon black pepper, freshly ground
- 1 piece lemongrass, bruised, 4 inch, and white part only
- 2 cups butternut squash, cubed
- 2 cups broccoli, chopped
- 1 can coconut milk, 13 ½ ounces
- 1 cup vegetable broth, or chicken broth
- 1 pound whitefish fillets, firm
- ¼ cup fresh cilantro, chopped
- 1 scallion, sliced thin
- Lemon wedges

Directions:

1. Melt the coconut oil in a large pot over medium-high heat. Add the onion, garlic, ginger, curry powder, salt, and pepper. Sauté for 5 minutes.

2. Add the lemongrass, butternut squash, and broccoli. Sauté for 2 minutes more.

3. Stir in the coconut milk and vegetable broth and bring to a boil. Reduce the heat to simmer and add the fish. Cover the pot and simmer for 5 minutes, or until the fish is cooked through. Remove the lemongrass.

4. Into a serving bowl, ladle the curry. Garnish with the cilantro and scallion and serve with the lemon wedges.

Nutrition Info:

- Info Per Serving: Calories: 553 ;Fat: 39g ;Protein: 34g ;Carbs: 22g .

Speedy Cod With Lemon & Cilantro

Servings: 4
Cooking Time: 20 Minutes
Ingredients:

- 2 tbsp olive oil
- 4 cod fillets
- 1 tbsp chopped cilantro
- Sea salt and pepper to taste
- 1 lemon, juiced

Directions:

1. Warm the olive oil in a skillet over medium heat. Sprinkle the cod with salt and pepper. Place it in the skillet and cook for 6-10 minutes on all sides until the cod is opaque and the skin is golden and crisp. Pour lemon juice over the fish and cook for 1 more minute. Top with cilantro.

Nutrition Info:

- Info Per Serving: Calories: 250;Fat: 10g;Protein: 2g;Carbs: 2g.

Japanese Salmon Cakes

Servings: 2
Cooking Time: 15 Minutes
Ingredients:

- 1 beaten egg
- 1 cup canned wild salmon,
- 2 spring onions, chopped
- ½ tsp honey
- 1 lime, zested
- 2 tsp reduced-salt soy sauce
- 1 tsp wasabi powder
- 2 tbsp coconut oil
- 1 tbsp ginger, minced

Directions:

1. Combine the salmon, egg, ginger, and lime zest, spring onions in a bowl and mix with your hands. Shape the mixture into 4 patties. In a separate bowl, add wasabi powder, soy sauce, and honey and whisk until blended.
2. Warm the coconut oil over medium heat in a skillet and cook the patties for 4 minutes until firm and browned on each side. Glaze the top of each patty with the wasabi mixture and cook for another 15 seconds. Serve.

Nutrition Info:

- Info Per Serving: Calories: 550;Fat: 30g;Protein: 67g;Carbs: 4g.

Mediterranean Salmon

Servings: 4
Cooking Time: 15 Minutes
Ingredients:

- 4 salmon fillets
- 2 tbsp olive oil
- 1 rosemary sprig
- 1 cup cherry tomatoes
- 15 oz asparagus

Directions:

1. Pour 1 cup of water into the Instant Pot and insert the steamer rack. Place the salmon on the steamer rack skin side down, rub with rosemary, and arrange the asparagus on top. Seal the lid and cook on "Manual" for 4 minutes. Perform a quick pressure release and carefully open the lid. Add in the cherry tomatoes on top and cook for another 2 minutes. Perform a quick pressure release. Serve drizzled with olive oil.

Nutrition Info:

- Info Per Serving: Calories: 475;Fat: 32g;Protein: 43g;Carbs: 6g.

Clams In White Wine

Servings: 4
Cooking Time: 20 Minutes
Ingredients:

- ¼ cup white wine
- 2 cups veggie broth
- ¼ cup chopped basil
- ¼ cup olive oil
- 2 ½ lb glams
- 2 tbsp lemon juice
- 2 garlic cloves, minced

Directions:

1. Heat the olive oil in your Instant Pot on "Sauté". Add garlic and sauté for 2 minutes. Add wine, basil, lemon juice, and veggie broth. Bring the mixture to a boil and boil for one minute. Add your steaming basket, and place the clams inside. Close the lid and cook for 5 minutes on "Manual" on high pressure. Place the clams on a plate and drizzle with the cooking liquid. Enjoy!

Nutrition Info:

- Info Per Serving: Calories: 230;Fat: 15g;Protein: 16g;Carbs: 6g.

Shanghai Cod With Udon Noodles

Servings: 2
Cooking Time:10 Minutes
Ingredients:

* 3 heads bok choy
* 2 black cod fillets
* 2 cups chicken broth
* 2 cups udon noodles
* 1 carrot, sliced
* 1 green onion, thinly sliced
* 1 tsp coconut oil
* 1 tsp five-spice powder
* 1 tbsp olive oil
* 1 tbsp ginger, minced
* Black pepper to taste
* 1 tbsp rice wine
* 1 tsp low-sodium soy sauce
* 2 tsp cilantro, chopped
* 1 tsp sesame seeds

Directions:

1. Place soy sauce, rice wine, pepper, 1 cup of chicken broth, coconut oil, and spice blend in a bowl and stir to combine. Warm the olive oil in a large saucepan over medium heat and cook the bok choy, ginger, and carrot for about 2 minutes until the bok choy is green. Add the rest of the reserved chicken stock and heat through.

2. Add the udon noodles and stir, bringing to a simmer. Add the green onion and the fish and cook for 10-15 minutes until the fish is tender. Add the fish, noodles, and vegetables into serving bowls. Pour the broth over the top.Garnish with cilantro and sesame seeds. Serve.

Nutrition Info:

* Info Per Serving: Calories: 485;Fat: 15g;Protein: 36g;Carbs: 43g.

Shrimp & Egg Risotto

Servings: 6
Cooking Time: 40 Minutes
Ingredients:

* 4 cups water
* 4 garlic cloves, minced
* 2 eggs, beaten
* ½ tsp grated ginger
* 3 tbsp olive oil
* ¼ tsp cayenne pepper
* 1 ½ cups frozen peas
* 2 cups brown rice
* ¼ cup soy sauce

* 1 cup chopped onion
* 12 oz peeled shrimp, thawed

Directions:

1. Heat the olive oil in your Instant Pot on "Sauté". Add the onion and garlic and cook for 2 minutes. Stir in the remaining ingredients except for the shrimp and eggs.

2. Close the lid and cook on "Manual" for 20 minutes. Wait about 10 minutes before doing a quick release. Stir in the shrimp and eggs. And let them heat for a couple of seconds with the lid off. Serve and enjoy!

Nutrition Info:

* Info Per Serving: Calories: 220;Fat: 10g;Protein: 13g;Carbs: 20g.

Crusty And Nutty Tilapia With Kale

Servings: 2
Cooking Time: 15 Minutes
Ingredients:

* 2 teaspoon extra virgin olive oil
* 2 tablespoon low fat hard cheese, grated
* ½ cup roasted and ground brazil nuts/hazelnuts/hard nut
* ½ cup bread crumbs, 100% wholegrain
* 2 tilapia fillets, skinless
* 2 teaspoons mustard, whole grain
* 1 head of kale, chopped
* 1 tablespoon sesame seeds, lightly toasted
* 1 clove of garlic, mashed

Directions:

1. Preheat the oven to 350°F.
2. Lightly oil a baking sheet with 1 teaspoon extra virgin olive oil.
3. In a separate bowl, mix in the nuts, breadcrumbs, and cheese.
4. Spread a thin layer of the mustard over the fish and then dip into the breadcrumb mixture.
5. Transfer to a baking dish.
6. Bake for 12 minutes or until cooked through.
7. In a skillet, heat 1 teaspoon oil on a medium heat and sauté the garlic for 30 seconds, adding in the kale for 5 minutes more.
8. Mix in the sesame seeds.
9. Serve the fish at once with the kale on the side.

Nutrition Info:

* Info Per Serving: Calories: 451 ;Fat: 31g Protein: 35g ;;Carbs: 14g.

A Must-try Spicy Sea Bass Fillets With Ginger

Servings: 2

Cooking Time: 10 Minutes

Ingredients:

- 2 sea bass fillets
- 1 teaspoon black pepper
- 1 tablespoon extra-virgin olive oil
- 1 teaspoon ginger, peeled and chopped
- 1 garlic clove, thinly sliced
- 1 red chili, deseeded and thinly sliced
- 2 green onion stems, sliced

Directions:

1. Get a skillet and heat the oil on a medium to high heat.
2. Sprinkle black pepper over the Sea Bass and score the skin of the fish a few times with a sharp knife.
3. Add the sea bass fillet to the very hot pan with the skin side down.
4. For 5 minutes, cook and turn over.
5. Cook for 2 minutes more.
6. Remove seabass from the pan and rest.
7. Add the chili, garlic and ginger and cook for 2 minutes or until golden.
8. Remove from the heat and add the green onions.
9. Scatter the vegetables over your sea bass to serve.
10. Try with a steamed sweet potato or side salad.

Nutrition Info:

- Info Per Serving: Calories: 159 ;Fat: 6g ;Protein: 24g ;Carbs: 2g .

Mushroom & Olive Cod Fillets

Servings: 4

Cooking Time: 35 Minutes

Ingredients:

- 4 cod fillets
- 1 garlic clove, minced
- 1 leek, thinly sliced
- 1 tsp minced fresh ginger
- 8 stoned black olives, sliced
- 1 tbsp olive oil
- ½ cup dry white wine
- ½ cup sliced mushrooms
- Sea salt and pepper to taste

Directions:

1. Preheat your oven to 375ºF. Combine the garlic, leek, ginger root, wine, olive oil, olives, and mushrooms in a baking pan, and toss until the mushrooms are evenly coated. Bake in the preheated oven for 10 minutes until lightly browned. Remove the baking pan from the oven. Spread the cod fillets on top and season with salt and pepper. Cover with aluminum foil and add back to the oven. Bake for 5-8 more minutes, or until the fish is flaky. Remove the foil and cool for 5 minutes before serving.

Nutrition Info:

- Info Per Serving: Calories: 165;Fat: 8g;Protein: 20g;Carbs: 5g.

Almond-crusted Tilapia

Servings: 4

Cooking Time: 20 Minutes

Ingredients:

- 4 tilapia fillets
- 2 tbsp sliced almonds
- 2 tbsp Dijon mustard
- 1 tsp olive oil
- ¼ tsp black pepper

Directions:

1. Pour 1 cup of water in your Instant Pot. Mix the olive oil, pepper, and mustard in a small bowl. Brush the fish fillets with the mustardy mixture on all sides. Coat the fish in almonds slices. Place the rack in your pot and arrange the fish fillets on it. Close the lid and cook for 5 minutes on "Manual" setting on High pressure. Do a quick pressure release and serve immediately.

Nutrition Info:

- Info Per Serving: Calories: 330;Fat: 15g;Protein: 46g;Carbs: 4g.

Hazelnut Crusted Trout Fillets

Servings: 4

Cooking Time: 30 Minutes

Ingredients:

- 4 boneless trout fillets
- 1 cup hazelnuts, ground
- 1 tbsp coconut oil, melted
- 2 tbsp chopped thyme
- Sea salt and pepper to taste
- Lemon wedges, for garnish

Directions:

1. Preheat your oven to 375ºF. Place the trout fillets on a greased baking sheet skin-side down. Season with salt and pepper. Gently press ¼ cup of ground hazelnuts into the flesh of each fillet. Drizzle the melted coconut oil over the nuts and then sprinkle with thyme. Bake for 15 minutes, or until the fish is cooked through. Serve.

Nutrition Info:

- Info Per Serving: Calories: 670;Fat: 59g;Protein: 29g;Carbs: 15g.

Hawaiian Tuna

Servings: 4
Cooking Time: 35 Minutes
Ingredients:
- 2 lb tuna, cubed
- 1 cup pineapple chunks
- ¼ cup chopped cilantro
- 2 tbsp chopped parsley
- 2 garlic cloves, minced
- 1 tbsp coconut oil
- 1 tbsp coconut aminos
- Sea salt and pepper to taste

Directions:

1. Preheat your oven to 400ºF. Add the tuna, pineapple, cilantro, parsley, garlic, coconut aminos, salt, and pepper to a baking dish and stir to coat. Bake for 15-20 minutes, or until the fish feels firm to the touch. Serve warm.

Nutrition Info:

- Info Per Serving: Calories: 410;Fat: 15g;Protein: 59g;Carbs: 7g.

Vegetarian Mains

Seitan Cauliflower Gratin

Servings: 4
Cooking Time: 40 Minutes
Ingredients:

- 2 tbsp olive oil
- 1 leek, coarsely chopped
- 1 white onion, chopped
- 2 cups broccoli florets
- 1 cup cauliflower florets
- 2 cups crumbled seitan
- 1 cup coconut cream
- 2 tbsp mustard powder
- 5 oz grated Parmesan
- 4 tbsp fresh rosemary
- Sea salt and pepper to taste

Directions:

1. Preheat your oven to 450ºF. Warm the olive oil in a pan over medium heat. Add the leek, white onion, broccoli, and cauliflower and cook for about 6 minutes. Transfer the vegetables to a baking dish. In the same pan, cook the seitan until browned. Mix the coconut cream and mustard powder in a bowl. Pour the mixture over the vegetables. Scatter the seitan and Parmesan cheese on top and sprinkle with rosemary, salt, and pepper. Bake for 15 minutes. Cool for a few minutes and serve.

Nutrition Info:

- Info Per Serving: Calories: 605;Fat: 39g;Protein: 19g;Carbs: 37g.

Distinctive Latino Stew With Black Bean

Servings: 4
Cooking Time: 25 Minutes
Ingredients:

- 1 cup brown rice, freshly cooked
- 1 cup quinoa, freshly cooked
- ½ cup of black olives, halved
- ½ cup black beans, cooked
- 1 avocado, sliced
- 2 tablespoons plain non-fat Greek yogurt
- ½ red onion, finely chopped
- 1 lime, juiced
- 1 lime, cut into wedges
- 1 tablespoon fresh cilantro, finely chopped

Directions:

1. Heat a pan of water on high heat and add brown rice for 15 minutes.
2. Heat a separate pan of water on high heat and add quinoa for 15 minutes.
3. Add the black beans to the pan of rice to cook along with the rice.
4. Check if most of the water in each pan has been absorbed, drain, and cover on the heat for 2 minutes. Turn off heat.
5. Grab a large serving bowl and mix rice, quinoa, beans, olives, red onion, tomato, and lime juice together.
6. Crush the avocado in a separate bowl into the yogurt with a fork and squeeze any remaining lime juice into the dip.
7. Enjoy your authentic Mexican meal, topped with cilantro, the avocado dip, and the lime wedges to serve.

Nutrition Info:

- Info Per Serving: Calories: 343 ;Fat: 12g ;Protein: 12g ;Carbs: 50g .

Mushroom Pizza

Servings: 4
Cooking Time: 35 Minutes
Ingredients:

- 1 cup chopped button mushrooms
- ½ cup sliced mixed bell peppers
- 2 tsp olive oil
- Sea salt and pepper to taste
- 1 whole-wheat pizza crust
- 1 cup tomato sauce
- 1 cup grated Parmesan
- 4 basil leaves

Directions:

1. Warm the olive oil in a skillet and sauté mushrooms and bell peppers for 10 minutes until softened. Season with salt and black pepper. Put the pizza crust on a pizza pan, spread the tomato sauce all over, and scatter vegetables evenly on top. Sprinkle with Parmesan. Bake for 20 minutes until the cheese has melted. Garnish with basil.

Nutrition Info:

- Info Per Serving: Calories: 420;Fat: 24g;Protein: 30g;Carbs: 39g.

Vegetable & Hummus Pizza

Servings: 4

Cooking Time: 30 Minutes

Ingredients:

- 10 mushrooms, sliced
- 3 ½ cups whole-wheat flour
- 1 tsp yeast
- 1 tsp sea salt
- 1 pinch sugar
- 3 tbsp olive oil
- 1 cup hummus
- ½ cup baby spinach
- 16 cherry tomatoes, halved
- ½ cup sliced black olives
- ½ medium onion, sliced
- 2 tsp dried oregano

Directions:

1. Preheat your oven the 350ºF and lightly grease a pizza pan with cooking spray. In a medium bowl, mix the flour, nutritional yeast, salt, sugar, olive oil, and 1 cup warm water until smooth dough forms. Allow rising for an hour or until the dough doubles in size. Spread the dough on the pizza pan and apply the hummus to the dough. Add the mushrooms, spinach, tomatoes, olives, onion, and top with the oregano. Bake for 20 minutes. Cool for 5 minutes, slice, and serve.

Nutrition Info:

- Info Per Serving: Calories: 600;Fat: 20g;Protein: 18g;Carbs: 94g.

Rice, Lentil & Spinach Pilaf

Servings: 4

Cooking Time: 25 Minutes

Ingredients:

- ½ cup wild rice
- 1 can lentils
- 1 can diced tomatoes
- 1 tsp dried thyme
- Sea salt and pepper to taste
- 3 cups baby spinach

Directions:

1. In a pot over medium heat, bring the rice and 1 ½ cups of salted water to a boil. Reduce the heat, cover, and simmer for 20 minutes. Add in lentils, tomatoes, thyme, salt, and pepper. Stir and cook until heated through. Mix in the spinach, cook for 2 minutes until the spinach wilts.

Nutrition Info:

- Info Per Serving: Calories: 135;Fat: 1g;Protein: 8g;Carbs: 28g.

Tofu Cabbage Stir-fry

Servings: 4

Cooking Time: 45 Minutes

Ingredients:

- 2 ½ cups bok choy, sliced
- 2 tbsp coconut oil
- 2 cups tofu, cubed
- 1 tsp garlic powder
- 1 tsp onion powder
- 1 tbsp plain vinegar
- 2 garlic cloves, minced
- 1 tsp chili flakes
- 1 tbsp grated ginger
- 3 green onions, sliced
- 1 tbsp olive oil
- 1 cup paleo mayonnaise

Directions:

1. Warm the coconut oil in a wok over medium heat. Add bok choy and stir-fry until softened. Season with salt, pepper, garlic powder, onion powder, and plain vinegar. Sauté for 2 minutes; set aside. To the wok, add the garlic, chili flakes, and ginger and sauté them until fragrant. Put the tofu in the wok and cook until browned on all sides. Add the green onions and bok choy, heat for 2 minutes, and add the olive oil. Stir in mayonnaise. Serve.

Nutrition Info:

- Info Per Serving: Calories: 200;Fat: 16g;Protein: 9g;Carbs: 6g.

Basil Pesto Seitan Panini

Servings: 4

Cooking Time: 15 Minutes + Cooling Time

Ingredients:

- For the seitan:
- 2/3 cup basil pesto
- ½ lemon, juiced
- 1 garlic clove, minced
- Sea salt to taste
- 1 cup chopped seitan
- For the panini:
- 3 tbsp basil pesto
- 8 whole-wheat ciabatta slices
- Olive oil for brushing
- 8 slices tofu
- 1 red bell pepper, chopped

- ¼ cup grated Parmesan

Directions:

1. In a bowl, mix pesto, lemon juice, garlic, and salt. Add the seitan and coat well with the marinade. Cover with plastic wrap and place in the refrigerator for 30 minutes. Preheat a skillet over medium heat and remove the seitan from the fridge. Cook the seitan in the skillet until brown and cooked through, 2-3 minutes. Turn the heat off.

2. Preheat a panini press to medium heat. In a small bowl, mix the pesto in the inner parts of two slices of bread. On the outer parts, apply some olive oil and place a slice with (the olive oil side down) in the press. Lay 2 slices of tofu on the bread, spoon some seitan on top. Sprinkle with some bell pepper and some Parmesan cheese. Cover with another bread slice. Close the press and grill the bread for 1 to 2 minutes. Flip the bread, and grill further for 1 minute or until the cheese melts and golden brown on both sides. Serve warm.

Nutrition Info:

- Info Per Serving: Calories: 780;Fat: 43g;Protein: 12g;Carbs: 80g.

Challenging Grain-free Fritters

Servings: 12
Cooking Time: 20 Minutes
Ingredients:

- 2 cups chickpea flour
- 1½ cups water
- 2 tablespoons chia seeds, ground
- ½ teaspoon salt
- 3 cups lightly packed spinach leaves, finely chopped
- 1 tablespoon coconut oil, or extra-virgin olive oil

Directions:

1. Whisk together the chickpea flour, water, chia seeds, and salt in a medium bowl. Ensure that there are no lumps by mixing it well.

2. Fold in the spinach.

3. Melt the coconut oil in a nonstick skillet set over medium-low heat.

4. Working in batches, use a ¼-cup measure to drop the batter into the pan. Flatten the fritters to about ½ inch thick. Don't crowd the pan.

5. Cook for 5 to 6 minutes. Flip the fritters and cook for 5 minutes more.

6. Transfer to a serving plate.

Nutrition Info:

- Info Per Serving: Calories: 318 ;Fat: 10g ;Protein: 15g ;Carbs: 45g .

Soft Zucchini With White Beans And Olives Stuffing

Servings: 4
Cooking Time: 20 Minutes
Ingredients:

- 4 large zucchinis, halved lengthwise
- 2 tablespoons extra-virgin olive oil, plus additional for brushing
- ½ teaspoon salt, plus additional for seasoning
- Freshly ground black pepper
- Pinch ground rosemary
- One 15 ounces can white beans, drained and rinsed
- ½ cup pitted green olives, chopped
- 2 garlic cloves, minced
- 1 cup arugula, coarsely chopped
- ¼ cup fresh parsley, chopped
- 1 tablespoon apple cider vinegar

Directions:

1. Preheat the oven to 375°F.

2. Brush a rimmed baking sheet with olive oil.

3. Carefully scoop out using a small spoon or melon baller and discard the seeds from the zucchini halves.

4. Brush the scooped-out section of each zucchini boat with olive oil and lightly season the inside of each boat with salt, pepper, and rosemary.

5. Transfer the zucchini to the prepared baking sheet, cut-side up. Place the sheet in the preheated oven and roast for 15 to 20 minutes, or until the zucchini are tender and lightly browned.

6. Lightly mash in a medium bowl the white beans with a fork.

7. Add the olives, garlic, arugula, parsley, cider vinegar, the remaining ½ teaspoon of salt, and the remaining 2 tablespoons of olive oil. Season with pepper and mix well.

8. Spoon the bean mixture into the zucchini boats and serve.

Nutrition Info:

- Info Per Serving: Calories: 269| Fat: 12g ;Protein: 13g ;Carbs: 38g.

Vegetarian Sloppy Joes

Servings: 4
Cooking Time: 30 Minutes
Ingredients:

- 2 tbsp avocado oil
- 2 garlic cloves, minced
- 1 yellow onion, chopped
- 1 celery stalk, chopped

- 1 carrot, minced
- ½ red bell pepper, chopped
- 1 lb cooked lentils
- 7 tbsp tomato paste
- 2 tbsp apple cider vinegar
- 1 tbsp maple syrup
- 1 tsp chili powder
- 1 tsp Dijon mustard
- ½ tsp dried oregano

Directions:

1. Warm 1 tbsp of avocado oil in a skillet over medium heat and place the garlic, carrot, onion, and celery and cook for 3 minutes until the onion is translucent. Add lentils and remaining avocado oil and cook for 5 more minutes.

2. Put in bell peppers and cook for 2 more minutes. Stir in tomato paste, apple cider vinegar, maple syrup, chili powder, Dijon mustard, and oregano and cook for another 10 minutes. Serve over rice.

Nutrition Info:

- Info Per Serving: Calories: 275;Fat: 8g;Protein: 14g;Carbs: 30g.

Hot Bean Salad

Servings: 4
Cooking Time: 45 Minutes

Ingredients:

- 1 cup pinto beans, soaked
- 4 tomatoes, sliced
- 2 celery stalks, sliced
- 2 red chilies, minced
- 2 chopped green onions
- 1 tbsp chopped parsley
- 2 tbsp olive oil
- 2 tbsp balsamic vinegar
- Sea salt and pepper to taste

Directions:

1. Cook pinto beans in salted water for 40 minutes. Drain and remove to a bowl. Let cool for a few minutes. Stir in tomatoes, celery, chilies, and green onions. In another bowl, mix olive oil, vinegar, salt, and pepper. Add the dressing to the bean bowl and toss to coat. Transfer to a serving plate. Top with parsley and serve.

Nutrition Info:

- Info Per Serving: Calories: 270;Fat: 8g;Protein: 11g;Carbs: 39g.

Veggie Burger Patties

Servings: 4
Cooking Time: 30 Minutes

Ingredients:

- 1 zucchini, grated
- 3 cups cauliflower florets
- 1 carrot, grated
- ½ cup veggie broth
- 2 cups broccoli florets
- ½ onion, diced
- ½ tsp turmeric powder
- 2 tbsp olive oil
- 2 cups sweet potato cubes
- ¼ tsp black pepper

Directions:

1. Heat 1 tablespoon of oil in your Instant Pot on "Sauté". Sauté the onions for about 3 minutes. Add carrots and cook for an additional minute. Add sweet potatoes and broth. Close the lid and cook on "Manual" for 10 minutes. Release the pressure quickly. Stir in the remaining veggies. Close the lid and cook for 3 more minutes on "Manual". Mash the veggies with a masher and stir in the seasonings. Let cool for a few minutes and make burger patties out of the mixture. Heat the rest of the oil. Cook the patties for about a minute on each side

Nutrition Info:

- Info Per Serving: Calories: 220;Fat: 7g;Protein: 3g;Carbs: 35g.

Feels Like Autumn Loaf With Root Vegetable

Servings: 6 To 8
Cooking Time: 55 Minutes To 1 Hour

Ingredients:

- 1 onion, finely chopped
- 2 tablespoons water
- 2 cups carrots, grated
- 1½ cups sweet potatoes, grated
- 1½ cups rolled oats, gluten-free
- ¾ cup butternut squash, purée
- 1 teaspoon salt

Directions:

1. Preheat the oven to 350°F.
2. Line a loaf pan with parchment paper.
3. Sauté the onion in the water in a large pot set over medium heat for 5 minutes, or until soft.
4. Add the carrots and sweet potatoes. Cook for 2 minutes. Remove the pot from the heat.
5. Stir in the oats, butternut squash purée, and salt. Mix well.

6. Transfer the mixture to the prepared loaf pan, pressing down evenly.

7. Place the pan in the preheated oven and bake for 50 to 55 minutes, uncovered, or until the loaf is firm and golden.

8. Cool for 10 minutes before slicing.

Nutrition Info:

- Info Per Serving: Calories: 169 ;Fat: 2g ;Protein: 5g ;Carbs: 34g .

Hot And Spicy Scrambled Tofu And Spinach

Servings: 2

Cooking Time: 10 Minutes

Ingredients:

- 1 pack extra firm tofu, pressed and crumbled
- 1 tablespoon of extra virgin olive oil
- 2 stems of spring onion, finely chopped
- 1 cup spinach leaves
- 1 clove of garlic, finely chopped
- 1 teaspoon lemon juice
- 1 teaspoon black pepper

Directions:

1. Heat olive oil in a skillet on medium heat.

2. Add the spring onion, tomatoes, and garlic and sauté for 3-4 minutes.

3. Lower the heat and add the tofu, lemon juice, and pepper.

4. Sauté for 3 to 5 minutes.

5. Turn the heat off and add the spinach then stir until spinach is wilted.

6. Transfer to a serving dish and enjoy.

Nutrition Info:

- Info Per Serving: Calories: 42 ;Fat: 3g ;Protein: 1g ;Carbs: 3g.

Pesto Mushroom Pizza

Servings: 4

Cooking Time: 40 Minutes

Ingredients:

- 1 cup sliced mushrooms
- 2 eggs
- ½ cup paleo mayonnaise
- ¾ cup whole-wheat flour
- 1 tsp baking powder
- 2 tbsp olive oil
- 1 tbsp basil pesto
- ½ cup red pizza sauce
- ¾ cup grated Parmesan

Directions:

1. Preheat your oven to 350ºF. Beat the eggs, mayonnaise, whole-wheat flour, baking powder, and salt in a bowl until dough forms. Spread the dough on a pizza pan and bake in the oven for 10 minutes or until the dough sets.

2. In a medium bowl, mix the mushrooms, olive oil, basil pesto, salt, and black pepper. Remove the pizza crust spread the pizza sauce on top. Scatter mushroom mixture on the crust and top with Parmesan cheese. Bake further until the cheese melts and the mushrooms soften, 10-15 minutes. Remove the pizza, slice, and serve.

Nutrition Info:

- Info Per Serving: Calories: 335;Fat: 20g;Protein: 16g;Carbs: 27g.

Hot Quinoa Florentine

Servings: 4

Cooking Time: 30 Minutes

Ingredients:

- ½ tsp crushed red pepper
- 2 tbsp olive oil
- 1 onion, chopped
- 3 cups fresh baby spinach
- 3 garlic cloves, minced
- 2 cups quinoa well
- 4 cups vegetable broth
- Sea salt and pepper to taste

Directions:

1. Warm the olive oil in a pot over medium heat, place the onion and spinach, and cook for 3 minutes. Stir in garlic and crushed red pepper and cook for another 30 seconds. Mix in quinoa, vegetable broth, salt, and pepper, bring to a boil, low the heat, and simmer for 15-20 minutes until the liquid is absorbed. Fluff the quinoa and serve.

Nutrition Info:

- Info Per Serving: Calories: 410;Fat: 13g;Protein: 8g;Carbs: 63g.

Watercress & Mushroom Spaghetti

Servings: 4

Cooking Time: 30 Minutes

Ingredients:

- ½ lb chopped button mushrooms
- 1 lb whole-wheat spaghetti
- 2 tbsp olive oil
- 2 shallots, chopped
- 2 garlic cloves, minced
- 4 tsp low-sodium soy sauce
- 1 tsp hot sauce

- A handful of watercress
- ¼ cup chopped parsley
- Sea salt and pepper to taste

Directions:

1. Cook spaghetti in lightly salted water in a large pot over medium heat until al dente, 10 minutes. Drain and set aside. Heat the olive oil in a skillet and sauté shallots, garlic, and mushrooms for 5 minutes. Stir in soy sauce, and hot sauce. Cook for 1 minute. Toss spaghetti in the sauce along with watercress and parsley. Season with black pepper. Dish the food and serve warm.

Nutrition Info:

- Info Per Serving: Calories: 485;Fat: 9g;Protein: 13g;Carbs: 90g.

Cheesy Cauliflower Casserole

Servings: 4

Cooking Time: 35 Minutes

Ingredients:

- 1 white onion, chopped
- ½ celery stalk, chopped
- 1 green bell pepper, chopped
- Sea salt and pepper to taste
- 1 head cauliflower, chopped
- 1 cup paleo mayonnaise
- 4 oz grated Parmesan
- 1 tsp red chili flakes

Directions:

1. Preheat your oven to 400ºF. Season onion, celery, and bell pepper with salt and black pepper. In a bowl, mix cauliflower, mayonnaise, Parmesan cheese, and red chili flakes. Pour the mixture into a greased baking dish and add the vegetables; mix to distribute. Bake for 20 minutes. Remove and serve warm.

Nutrition Info:

- Info Per Serving: Calories: 115;Fat: 4g;Protein: 17g;Carbs: 6g.

Appetizing Casserole With Broccoli And Bean

Servings: 4

Cooking Time: 35 To 45 Minutes

Ingredients:

- ¾ cup vegetable broth, or water
- 2 broccoli heads, crowns and stalks finely chopped
- 1 teaspoon salt
- 2 cups cooked pinto or navy beans, or One 14 ounces can

- 1 to 2 tablespoons brown rice flour, or arrowroot flour
- 1 cup walnuts, chopped

Directions:

1. Preheat the oven to 350°F.

2. Warm the broth in a large ovenproof pot set over medium heat.

3. Add the broccoli and salt. Cook for 6 to 8 minutes, or until the broccoli is bright green.

4. Stir in the pinto beans and brown rice flour. Cook for 5 minutes more, or until the liquid thickens slightly.

5. Sprinkle the walnuts over the top.

Nutrition Info:

- Info Per Serving: Calories: 410 ;Fat: 20g ;Protein: 22g ;Carbs: 43g.

Magical One-pot Tomato Basil Pasta

Servings: 4

Cooking Time: 10 Minutes

Ingredients:

- 2 tablespoons extra-virgin olive oil, plus additional for drizzling
- 1 onion, sliced thin
- 2 garlic cloves, sliced thin
- 1 pound penne pasta, gluten-free
- One 15 ounces can tomatoes, chopped
- 1½ teaspoons salt
- ¼ teaspoon black pepper, freshly ground
- ¼ cup chopped fresh basil, plus 4 whole basil leaves
- 4½ cups water

Directions:

1. Heat 2 tablespoons of olive oil in a large, heavy-bottomed Dutch oven over medium heat. Add the onion and garlic. Stir to coat with the oil.

2. Add the pasta, tomatoes, salt, pepper, the 4 whole basil leaves, and water to the pot. Bring the liquid to a boil and cover the pot. Cook for 8 to 10 minutes. Check the pasta to see if it is cooked and add more water if necessary. Cook until the pasta is tender.

3. Transfer the pasta to a serving bowl and garnish with the remaining ¼ cup of chopped basil and a drizzle of olive oil.

Nutrition Info:

- Info Per Serving: Calories: 518 ;Fat: 11g ;Protein: 10g ;Carbs: 95g.

Shallot & Mushroom Risotto

Servings: 4
Cooking Time: 25 Minutes
Ingredients:

- 1 cup arborio rice
- 2 cups vegetable broth
- 2 tbsp olive oil
- 1 shallot, sliced
- 10 mushrooms, sliced
- ½ cup dry red wine
- ½ cup Parmesan, grated
- 1 tbsp parsley, chopped
- Sea salt and pepper to taste

Directions:

1. Warm the olive oil in a skillet over medium heat. Place the shallot and cook for 3-5 minutes until softened. Add in mushrooms and red wine and simmer until the wine evaporates. Stir in arborio rice and cook for another 3 minutes. Pour in ½ cup of vegetable broth and cook until the liquid has absorbed, stirring often. Repeat the process for 20 minutes until the risotto is tender. Serve topped with parsley, Parmesan cheese, salt, and pepper.

Nutrition Info:

- Info Per Serving: Calories: 322;Fat: 12g;Protein: 10g;Carbs: 8g.

Tempeh Coconut Curry Bake

Servings: 4
Cooking Time: 30 Minutes
Ingredients:

- 2 ½ cups chopped tempeh
- Sea salt and pepper to taste
- 1 tbsp olive oil
- 2 tbsp red curry paste
- 1 ½ cups coconut cream
- ½ cup parsley, chopped
- 15 oz cauliflower florets

Directions:

1. Preheat your oven to 400ºF. Arrange the tempeh on a greased baking dish, sprinkle with salt and black pepper and drizzle each tempeh with olive oil. In a bowl, mix the red curry paste with coconut cream and parsley. Pour the mixture over the tempeh. Bake in the oven for 20 minutes or until the tempeh is cooked.

2. Season the cauliflower with salt, place in a microwave-safe bowl, and sprinkle with some water. Steam in the microwave for 3 minutes or until the cauliflower is soft and tender within. Remove and serve with tempeh.

Nutrition Info:

- Info Per Serving: Calories: 570;Fat: 47g;Protein: 25g;Carbs: 24g.

Scallion & Feta Fried Rice

Servings: 4
Cooking Time: 25 Minutes
Ingredients:

- 2 tbsp olive oil
- 8 oz feta cheese, crumbled
- 6 scallions, thinly sliced
- 2 cups kale, chopped
- 3 cups cooked brown rice
- ¼ cup stir-fry sauce

Directions:

1. Warm the olive oil in a skillet over medium heat and place in the scallions and kale; cook for 5-7 minutes until the veggies are tender. Mix in brown rice and stir-fry sauce and cook for 3-5 minutes until all heat through. Top with feta cheese and serve. Enjoy!

Nutrition Info:

- Info Per Serving: Calories: 300;Fat: 12g;Protein: 4g;Carbs: 37g.

Chipotle Kidney Bean Chili

Servings: 4
Cooking Time: 30 Minutes
Ingredients:

- 2 tbsp olive oil
- 1 onion, chopped
- 2 garlic cloves, minced
- 1 can tomato sauce
- 1 tbsp chili powder
- 1 chipotle chili, minced
- 1 tsp ground cumin
- ½ tsp dried marjoram
- 1 can kidney beans
- Sea salt and pepper to taste
- ½ tsp cayenne pepper

Directions:

1. Heat the oil in a pot over medium heat. Place in onion and garlic and sauté for 3 minutes. Put in tomato sauce, chipotle chili, chili powder, cumin, cayenne pepper, marjoram, salt, and pepper and cook for 5 minutes. Stir in kidney beans and 2 cups of water. Bring to a boil, then lower the heat and simmer for 15 minutes, stirring often.

Nutrition Info:

- Info Per Serving: Calories: 260;Fat: 11g;Protein: 6g;Carbs: 37g.

Sweet Potato Chili

Servings: 4

Cooking Time: 30 Minutes

Ingredients:

- 15 oz canned black beans
- 2 cups veggie broth
- 28 oz canned diced tomatoes
- 15 oz canned kidney beans
- 2 sweet potatoes, chopped
- 1 red onion, chopped
- 1 red bell pepper, chopped
- 1 green bell pepper, chopped
- 1 tbsp olive oil
- 1 tbsp chili powder
- ¼ tsp cinnamon
- 1 tsp cumin
- 2 tsp cocoa powder
- 1 tsp cayenne pepper
- Sea salt to taste

Directions:

1. Heat the olive oil in your Instant Pot on "Sauté". Add the onions, peppers, and sweet potatoes. Cook until the onions become translucent. Stir in the rest of the ingredients. Seal the lid and cook on "Manual" for 12 minutes. Once the cooking is complete, let the pressure release naturally for 5 minutes. Serve hot.

Nutrition Info:

- Info Per Serving: Calories: 300;Fat: 4g;Protein: 16g;Carbs: 55g.

Black Bean Burgers

Servings: 4

Cooking Time: 20 Minutes

Ingredients:

- 4 whole-grain hamburger buns, split
- 3 cans black beans
- 2 tbsp whole-wheat flour
- 2 tbsp quick-cooking oats
- ¼ cup chopped fresh basil
- 2 tbsp pure barbecue sauce
- 1 garlic clove, minced
- Sea salt and pepper to taste

Directions:

1. In a bowl, mash the black beans and mix in the flour, oats, basil, barbecue sauce, garlic salt, and black pepper until well combined. Mold patties out of the mixture.

2. Heat a grill pan to medium heat and lightly grease with cooking spray. Cook the bean patties on both sides until

light brown and cooked through, 10 minutes. Place the patties between the burger buns and garnish with your favorite topping. Serve warm.

Nutrition Info:

- Info Per Serving: Calories: 420;Fat: 4g;Protein: 4g;Carbs: 75g.

Curried Indian Rolls

Servings: 4

Cooking Time: 15 Minutes

Ingredients:

- 3 tbsp tahini
- Zest and juice of 1 lime
- 1 tbsp curry powder
- Sea salt to taste
- 1 can chickpeas
- 1 cup diced peaches
- 1 red bell pepper, diced small
- ½ cup cilantro, chopped
- 4 large whole-grain wraps
- 2 cups arugula

Directions:

1. In a bowl, beat tahini, lime zest, lime juice, curry powder, 3-4 tbsp of water, and salt until creamy. In another bowl, combine the chickpeas, peaches, bell pepper, cilantro, and tahini dressing. Divide the mixture between the wraps and top with arugula. Roll up and serve.

Nutrition Info:

- Info Per Serving: Calories: 535;Fat: 15g;Protein: 8g;Carbs: 84g.

Oozing Homemade Sushi With Avocado

Servings: 4

Cooking Time: 15 Minutes

Ingredients:

- 1½ cups dry quinoa
- 3 cups water, plus additional for rolling
- ½ teaspoon salt
- 6 nori sheets
- 3 avocados, halved, pitted, and sliced thin, divided
- 1 small cucumber, halved, seeded, and cut into matchsticks, divided

Directions:

1. In a fine-mesh sieve, rinse the quinoa.

2. Combine the rinsed quinoa, water, and salt in a medium pot set over high heat. Bring to a boil. Reduce the heat to

low. Cover and simmer for 15 minutes. Fluff the quinoa with a fork.

3. Lay out 1 nori sheet on a cutting board. Spread ½ cup of quinoa over the sheet, leaving 2 to 3 inches uncovered at the top.

4. Place 5 or 6 avocado slices across the bottom of the nori sheet in a row. Add 5 or 6 cucumber matchsticks on top.

5. Tightly roll up the nori sheet by starting at the bottom sheet. Dab the uncovered top with water to seal the roll.

6. Slice the sushi roll into 6 pieces.

7. Repeat with the remaining 5 nori sheets, quinoa, and vegetables.

8. Serve.

Nutrition Info:

- Info Per Serving: Calories: 557 ;Fat: 33g ;Protein: 13g ;Carbs: 57g .

Zucchini & Chickpea Casserole

Servings: 6
Cooking Time: 45 Minutes
Ingredients:

- 2 tbsp olive oil
- 1 tsp dried oregano
- 15 oz canned chickpeas
- 2 garlic cloves, minced
- 1 zucchini, chopped
- 1 onion, chopped
- ½ tsp ground cumin
- 4 eggs, beaten lightly
- Sea salt and pepper to taste

Directions:

1. Preheat your oven to 350°F. Warm 2 tbsp of olive oil in a skillet over high heat and place the garlic, onion, and zucchini and cook for 5 minutes until the veggies are brown. Set aside in a bowl. Place the chickpeas in the bowl with the veggies and mash them. Stir in oregano, cumin, eggs, salt, and pepper, pour it in a greased baking pan, and bake for 20 minutes. Let cool before serving.

Nutrition Info:

- Info Per Serving: Calories: 215;Fat: 10g;Protein: 10g;Carbs: 15g.

Spinach & Butternut Squash Curry

Servings: 4
Cooking Time: 30 Minutes
Ingredients:

- 2 tbsp olive oil
- 1 onion, chopped
- 1 lb cubed butternut squash
- 4 cups fresh baby spinach
- 3 cups vegetable broth
- 1 cup lite coconut milk
- 2 tbsp curry powder
- Sea salt and pepper to taste

Directions:

1. Warm the olive oil in a skillet over medium heat and place the onion. Cook for 5 minutes until soft. Mix in butternut squash, spinach, vegetable broth, coconut milk, curry powder, salt, and pepper and bring to a simmer. Cook for 15 minutes until the potatoes are tender. Serve.

Nutrition Info:

- Info Per Serving: Calories: 320;Fat: 12g;Protein: 10g;Carbs: 51g.

Sauces, Condiments, And Dressings

Healthy Vegan Buffalo Dip

Servings: 4 To 6

Cooking Time: 5 To 6 Hours

Ingredients:

- 1 pound cauliflower, chopped
- 1¼ cups raw cashews, soaked in water overnight, drained
- ¾ cup hot sauce
- ½ cup water
- 1 tablespoon lemon juice, freshly squeezed
- 1 teaspoon garlic powder
- ½ teaspoon paprika
- Sea salt
- Freshly ground black pepper
- Chopped veggies

Directions:

1. Combine the cauliflower, cashews, hot sauce, water, lemon juice, garlic powder, and paprika in your slow cooker. Season with salt and pepper.

2. Cover the cooker and set to low. Cook for 5 to 6 hours.

3. Transfer the mixture to a blender or food processor. Pulse until the preferred consistency is reached. Serve with chopped veggies.

Nutrition Info:

- Info Per Serving: Calories: 302 ;Fat: 18g ;Protein: 9g ;Carbs: 26g.

Lemony Honey With Ginger

Servings: 1

Cooking Time: 0 Minutes

Ingredients:

- 1 cup water
- ¼ cup lemon juice, fresh
- 2 tablespoons honey
- 2 teaspoons grated fresh ginger root

Directions:

1. In an airtight jar, combine all the ingredients and shake until the honey is dissolved.

2. Refrigerate for a day before using so the ginger can permeate the mixture.

3. Store in the refrigerator for up to a week.

Nutrition Info:

- Info Per Serving: Calories: 20 ;Fat: 15g;Protein: 46g;Carbs: 5g .

French Pistou

Servings: 1 ½

Cooking Time: 0 Minutes

Ingredients:

- 3 packed cups fresh basil leaves
- 6 cloves garlic, peeled
- ¾ cup avocado oil
- ½ cup hemp seeds, shelled
- 1 teaspoon Himalayan salt, fine
- 1 teaspoon garlic powder
- 1 teaspoon black pepper, ground

Directions:

1. Place all of the ingredients in a blender or food processor. Pulse until all of the basil and garlic is minced.

2. Blend on low for 20 to 30 seconds to smooth it out just a bit and bring the texture of the sauce together. Use a spatula to scrape it all out into a glass jar with a lid. Store in the fridge for up to 10 days.

Nutrition Info:

- Info Per Serving: Calories: 490 ;Fat: 47g ;Protein: 14g;Carbs: 5g .

Sweet Jam With Strawberry And Chia

Servings: 1

Cooking Time: 8 To 10 Minutes

Ingredients:

- 3 cups fresh strawberries, hulled and halved
- ¼ cup maple syrup, or raw honey
- 3 tablespoons chia seeds

Directions:

1. Cook in a large pot set over medium-low heat the strawberries for 8 to 10 minutes. Mash them lightly with a fork. Add 1 or 2 tablespoons of water if the pan gets dry. Transfer to a blender.

2. Add the maple syrup. Blend until smooth. Pour the mixture into a medium bowl.

3. Stir in the chia seeds.

4. Transfer the jam to a jar. Cover and refrigerate. It will thicken as it cools.

Nutrition Info:

- Info Per Serving: Calories: 30 ;Fat: 1g ;Protein: 1g ;Carbs: 7g .

Must-have Ranch Dressing

Servings: 1 ½

Cooking Time: 0 Minutes

Ingredients:

- ½ cup water, filtered
- ½ cup coconut milk, full-fat
- ½ cup hemp seeds, shelled
- 2 tablespoons red wine vinegar
- 1 tablespoon coconut aminos
- 1 tablespoon Dijon mustard
- 2 teaspoons dill weed, dried
- 1 teaspoon parsley, dried
- 1 teaspoon Himalayan salt, fine
- 1 teaspoon fish sauce
- 1 teaspoon garlic powder
- 1 teaspoon onion powder
- 1 teaspoon black pepper, ground

Directions:

1. Place all of the ingredients in a blender and blend until smooth.

2. Store in an airtight glass or ceramic container in the fridge for up to 10 days. Before using, set out at room temperature to soften for a few minutes and shake or stir to mix well.

Nutrition Info:

- Info Per Serving: Calories: 225 ;Fat: 18g ;Protein: 11g;Carbs: 4g.

Natural Dressing With Ginger And Turmeric

Servings: ½

Cooking Time: 0 Minutes

Ingredients:

- 1 cup extra-virgin olive oil
- ¼ cup apple cider vinegar
- ½ teaspoon Dijon mustard
- 1 garlic clove, sliced
- ½ teaspoon fresh ginger root, minced
- 1 teaspoon salt
- ½ teaspoon turmeric, ground
- ¼ teaspoon coriander, ground
- ¼ teaspoon black pepper, freshly ground

Directions:

1. Combine all the ingredients in a blender or food processor and process until smooth.

2. Refrigerate in an airtight container for up to a week.

Nutrition Info:

- Info Per Serving: Calories: 160 ;Fat: 18g; Protein: 46g;Carbs: 4g.

Tasty And Fiery Tunisian Vinaigrette

Servings: 1 ¼

Cooking Time: 0 Minutes

Ingredients:

- ¾ cup olive oil
- ¼ cup apple cider vinegar
- 1 tablespoon lemon juice, freshly squeezed
- ¼ cup fresh parsley, chopped
- 1 teaspoon minced garlic, bottled
- 1 teaspoon cumin, ground
- ¼ teaspoon coriander, ground
- Pinch sea salt

Directions:

1. Whisk the olive oil, cider vinegar, and lemon juice in a medium bowl until emulsified.

2. Whisk in the parsley, garlic, cumin, and coriander.

3. Season with sea salt.

4. Refrigerate the vinaigrette in a sealed container for up to 2 weeks.

Nutrition Info:

- Info Per Serving: Calories: 133 ;Fat: 15g;Protein: 26g;Carbs: 4g.

Old Fashioned Dressing With Lemon And Mustard

Servings: 1 ½

Cooking Time: 0 Minutes

Ingredients:

- 1 cup extra-virgin olive oil
- ¼ cup lemon juice, fresh
- 1 tablespoon honey
- 1 teaspoon Dijon mustard
- 1 shallot, sliced
- 1 teaspoon lemon zest, grated
- 1 teaspoon salt
- ¼ teaspoon pepper

Directions:

1. Combine the olive oil, lemon juice, honey, Dijon, shallot, lemon zest, salt, and pepper in a blender or food processor. Process until smooth.

2. Refrigerate in an airtight container for up to 5 days.

Nutrition Info:

- Info Per Serving: Calories: 180 ;Fat: 20g ;Protein: 16g;Carbs: 2g .

Awesome Multi-purpose Cream Sauce

Servings: 3 ½
Cooking Time: 12 Minutes
Ingredients:
- 3 cups cubed butternut squash
- ½ cup cashews, soaked in water for 4 hours, drained
- ½ cup water, plus additional for cooking and thinning
- 1 teaspoon salt, plus additional as needed

Directions:
1. Fill a large pot with 2 inches of water and insert a steamer basket. Bring to a boil over high heat.
2. Add the butternut squash to the basket. Cover and steam for 10 to 12 minutes or until tender.
3. Remove from the heat and cool slightly.
4. Transfer the squash to a blender. Add the cashews, ½ cup of water, and salt. Blend until smooth and creamy. Add more water depending on the consistency to thin if necessary.
5. Taste and adjust the seasoning if needed.

Nutrition Info:
- Info Per Serving: Calories: 73 ;Fat: 5g ;Protein: 2g ;Carbs: 8g .

Marinated Greek Dressing

Servings: 1 ½
Cooking Time: 0 Minutes
Ingredients:
- 3 cloves garlic, minced
- 1 cup extra-virgin olive oil or avocado oil
- Juice of 3 lemons, ½ cup
- 2 tablespoons fresh oregano leaves, minced
- 1 teaspoon black pepper, ground
- 1 teaspoon onion powder
- ½ teaspoon Himalayan salt, fine

Directions:
1. In a blender, place all of the ingredients and blend on medium speed until the dressing has emulsified and has a light-brown appearance and the garlic is almost smooth.
2. Store in an airtight container in the fridge for up to 10 days. Shake or stir before using since this. dressing separates very quickly

Nutrition Info:
- Info Per Serving: Calories: 150 ;Fat: 17g ;Protein: 46g;Carbs: 1g .

Garlicky Sauce With Tahini

Servings: 1
Cooking Time: 0 Minutes

Ingredients:
- ½ cup tahini
- 1 garlic clove, minced
- Juice of 1 lemon
- Zest of 1 lemon
- ½ teaspoon salt, plus additional as needed
- ½ cup warm water, plus additional as needed

Directions:
1. Stir together in a small bowl the tahini and garlic.
2. Add the lemon juice, lemon zest, and salt. Stir well.
3. Whisk in ½ cup of warm water, until fully mixed and creamy. Add more water if the sauce is too thick.
4. Taste and adjust the seasoning if needed.
5. Refrigerate in a sealed container.

Nutrition Info:
- Info Per Serving: Calories: 180 ;Fat: 16g ;Protein: 5g ;Carbs: 7g .

Herbaceous Spread With Avocado

Servings: 2
Cooking Time: 0minutes
Ingredients:
- 1 avocado, peeled and pitted
- 2 tablespoons lemon juice, freshly squeezed
- 2 tablespoons fresh parsley, chopped
- 1 teaspoon fresh dill, chopped
- ½ teaspoon coriander, ground
- Sea salt
- Freshly ground black pepper

Directions:
1. Pulse the avocado in a blender until smoothly puréed.
2. Add the lemon juice, parsley, dill, and coriander. Pulse until well blended.
3. Season with sea salt and pepper.
4. Refrigerate the spread in a sealed container for up to 4 days.

Nutrition Info:
- Info Per Serving: Calories: 53 ;Fat: 5g ;Protein: 1g;Carbs: 2g .

Fragrant Peach Butter

Servings: 2
Cooking Time: 3 Hours
Ingredients:
- Eight 3 pounds peaches, peeled, pitted, and chopped, or about 6 cups frozen, sliced peaches
- Water
- ¼ cup raw honey

Directions:

1. Combine in a large saucepan over high heat the peaches with enough water to cover the fruit by about 1 inch. Bring the liquid to a boil.

2. Reduce the heat to low and simmer for 3 hours while stirring frequently until the mixture appears a thick applesauce.

3. Stir in the honey. Simmer for 30 minutes until the mixture starts to caramelize. Remove the peach butter from the heat and let it cool for 30 minutes.

4. Spoon the mixture into a container and cool completely before covering. Keep refrigerated for up to 2 weeks.

Nutrition Info:

- Info Per Serving: Calories: 46 ;Fat: 15g;Protein: 1g;Carbs: 11g .

Great On Everything Ginger Sauce

Servings: 1 ½
Cooking Time: 0 Minutes
Ingredients:

- ½ cup full-fat coconut milk
- ¼ cup coconut aminos
- ¼ cup fresh ginger, peeled and minced
- 4 cloves garlic, peeled
- 2 tablespoons coconut vinegar or red wine vinegar
- 2 tablespoons sesame oil
- 1 tablespoon Dijon mustard
- 1 tablespoon fish sauce
- 1 teaspoon minced lemongrass or grated lemon zest

Directions:

1. Place all of the ingredients in a blender and blend on high until the mixture is smooth and light brown.

2. Store in an airtight container in the refrigerator for up to 10 days. Shake before using.

Nutrition Info:

- Info Per Serving: Calories: 113 ;Fat: 10g ;Protein: 1g;Carbs: 6g .

Verde Chimichurri With Parsley

Servings: 1
Cooking Time: 0 Minutes
Ingredients:

- 1 cup coarsely fresh parsley, chopped
- ½ cup fresh mint leaves
- ¼ cup olive oil
- 2 tablespoons lemon juice, freshly squeezed
- 2 teaspoons minced garlic, bottled
- Pinch sea salt

Directions:

1. Combine the parsley, mint, olive oil, lemon juice, garlic, and sea salt in a blender or food processor. Pulse until finely chopped and the ingredients are well mixed.

2. Refrigerate the mixture in a sealed container for up to 1 week.

Nutrition Info:

- Info Per Serving: Calories: 61 ;Fat: 6g ;Protein: 1g;Carbs: 1g .

Colourful And Sweet Spread With Carrot

Servings: 2
Cooking Time: 0 Minutes
Ingredients:

- 3 carrots, peeled and cut into chunks
- ½ cup almonds
- 2 tablespoons lemon juice, freshly squeezed
- 1 tablespoon pure maple syrup
- ½ teaspoon cardamom, ground
- Sea salt

Directions:

1. Pulse the carrots until very finely chopped in a food processor.

2. Add the almonds, lemon juice, maple syrup, and cardamom then process until smooth.

3. Season the spread with sea salt and transfer to a lidded container. Refrigerate for up to 6 days.

Nutrition Info:

- Info Per Serving: Calories: 26 ;Fat: 2g ;Protein: 1g;Carbs: 3g ,

Colourful Fiesta Guacamole

Servings: 3
Cooking Time: 0 Minutes
Ingredients:

- 3 medium Hass avocados, halved, pitted, and peeled
- 3 small radishes, sliced
- 3 large strawberries, diced
- 3 cloves garlic, minced
- 1 green onion, sliced
- ½ bunch fresh cilantro, minced and 1½ ounces
- Juice of 2 lemons
- 2 teaspoons Himalayan salt, fine
- 1 tablespoon extra-virgin olive oil

Directions:

1. In a large bowl, place all the ingredients. Use a whisk or pestle to mix and mash them together until you have chunky guacamole.

2. Transfer it to an airtight container, drizzle olive oil on it, set a sheet of plastic wrap on the top so that it sticks directly to the guacamole, and put the lid on. Store in the fridge until ready to enjoy, but no more than 4 days.

Nutrition Info:

*   Info Per Serving: Calories: 215 ;Fat: 18g ;Protein: 4g;Carbs: 15g .

Traditional And Delightful Gremolata Sauce

Servings: 1
Cooking Time: 0 Minutes

Ingredients:

*   ¾ cup finely fresh parsley, chopped
*   Juice of 2 lemons or 6 tablespoons
*   Zest of 2 lemons
*   2 tablespoons olive oil
*   2 teaspoons minced garlic, bottled
*   ¼ teaspoon sea salt

Directions:

1. Stir together in a small bowl the parsley, lemon juice, lemon zest, olive oil, garlic, and sea salt until well blended.
2. Refrigerate in a sealed container for up to 4 days.

Nutrition Info:

*   Info Per Serving: Calories: 33 ;Fat: 4g ;Protein: 46g;Carbs: 1g.

Slow Cooked Caramelized Onions

Servings: 2
Cooking Time: 10 Hours

Ingredients:

*   4 large onions (white or sweet), sliced very thin
*   2 tablespoons extra-virgin olive oil
*   ½ teaspoon sea salt

Directions:

1. Combine in your slow cooker the onions, olive oil, and salt. Stir to coat the onions with the oil.
2. Cover the cooker and set it to low. Cook for 10 hours. Drain the liquid then serve.

Nutrition Info:

*   Info Per Serving: Calories: 234 ;Fat: 14g ;Protein: 3g ;Carbs: 26g .

Gluten Free Apple Chutney

Servings: 2
Cooking Time: 10 Minutes

Ingredients:

*   1 tablespoon almond oil
*   4 apples, peeled, cored, and diced
*   1 small onion, diced
*   ½ cup white raisins
*   1 tablespoon apple cider vinegar
*   1 tablespoon honey
*   1 teaspoon cinnamon, ground
*   ½ teaspoon cardamom, ground
*   ½ teaspoon ginger, ground
*   ½ teaspoon salt

Directions:

1. Heat in a medium saucepan the oil over low heat.
2. Add the apples, onion, raisins6, vinegar, honey, cinnamon, cardamom, ginger, and salt. Cook briefly until the apples release their juices. Bring to a simmer, cover, and cook until the apples are tender for 5 to 10 minutes.
3. Allow to cool completely before serving.

Nutrition Info:

*   Info Per Serving: Calories: 120 ;Fat: 2g ;Protein: 1g ;Carbs: 24g .

Delicious Pesto With Kale

Servings: 1
Cooking Time: 0 Minutes

Ingredients:

*   2 cups chopped kale leaves, thoroughly washed and stemmed
*   ½ cup almonds, toasted
*   2 garlic cloves
*   3 tablespoons lemon juice, freshly squeezed
*   3 tablespoons extra-virgin olive oil
*   2 teaspoons lemon zest
*   1 teaspoon salt
*   ½ teaspoon black pepper, freshly ground
*   ¼ teaspoon red pepper flakes

Directions:

1. Combine in a food processor the kale, almonds, garlic, lemon juice, olive oil, lemon zest, salt, black pepper, and red pepper flakes then process until smooth.
2. Refrigerate in an airtight container for up to one week.

Nutrition Info:

*   Info Per Serving: Calories: 91 ;Fat: 8g ;Protein: 2g;Carbs: 4g .

Goddess And Vibrant Green Dressing

Servings: 2
Cooking Time: 0 Minutes
Ingredients:

- 4 cloves garlic, peeled
- ½ cup fresh chives or green onions, minced
- ¼ cup lemon juice
- 2 tablespoons coconut aminos
- 1 tablespoon Dijon mustard
- 1½ teaspoons Himalayan salt, fine
- 1 teaspoon chia seeds
- 1 teaspoon black pepper, ground
- 1 teaspoon poppy seeds
- 1 teaspoon hemp seeds, shelled
- 5 drops liquid stevia
- 1 cup avocado oil

Directions:

1. Place all of the ingredients except the oil in a blender and pulse to combine. Drizzle slowly in the avocado oil while the blender runs until the sauce comes creamy and smooth.
2. Store in an airtight container in the refrigerator for up to 10 days. Shake before using.

Nutrition Info:

- Info Per Serving: Calories: 128 ;Fat: 14g ;Protein: 4g;Carbs: 1g.

Satisfying And Thick Dressing With Avocado

Servings: 2
Cooking Time: 0 Minutes
Ingredients:

- 1 ripe avocado
- 1 cup coconut yogurt, plain
- ¼ cup lemon juice, freshly squeezed
- 1 scallion, chopped
- 1 tablespoon fresh cilantro, chopped

Directions:

1. Blend in a food processor the avocado, yogurt, lemon juice, scallion, and cilantro until smooth.
2. Refrigerate in an airtight container.

Nutrition Info:

- Info Per Serving: Calories: 33 ;Fat: 3g ;Protein: 8g;Carbs: 2g .

Decadent And Simple Alfredo With Cauliflower

Servings: 2
Cooking Time: 12 Minutes
Ingredients:

- 3 cups cauliflower, florets
- 5 cloves garlic, peeled
- 1 cup coconut milk, full-fat
- 3 tablespoons salted butter, ghee, or lard
- 1 tablespoon fish sauce
- 1 tablespoon red wine vinegar
- 1 teaspoon Himalayan salt, fine
- 1 teaspoon black pepper, ground

Directions:

1. Fill a saucepan with about an inch of water and add the cauliflower and garlic. Heat the pan over medium-high heat and bring to a boil with the lid on. Cook for 8 minutes until the cauliflower is fork-tender. Remove from the heat and drain.
2. In a blender, place the cauliflower, garlic, and remaining ingredients. Purée until smooth.
3. Store in an airtight container in the fridge for up to 10 days. Bring to a simmer in a saucepan over medium heat to reheat.

Nutrition Info:

- Info Per Serving: Calories: 250 ;Fat: 24g ;Protein: 4g ;Carbs: 9g .

Fantastic On Hand Marinara Sauce

Servings: 6
Cooking Time: 7 To 8 Hours
Ingredients:

- 2 cans diced tomatoes, 28 ounces
- 3 tablespoons tomato paste
- 1 yellow onion, diced
- 1 carrot, minced
- 1 celery stalk, minced
- 2 bay leaves
- 1 tablespoon basil leaves, dried
- 2 teaspoons oregano, dried
- 1½ teaspoons garlic powder
- 1 teaspoon sea salt
- Pinch red pepper flakes
- Freshly ground black pepper

Directions:

1. Combine in your slow cooker the tomatoes, tomato paste, onion, carrot, celery, bay leaves, basil, oregano, garlic

powder, salt, and red pepper flakes, and season with black pepper.

2. Cover the cooker and set it to low. Cook for 7 to 8 hours.

3. Remove and discard the bay leaves. Blend using an immersion blender the sauce to your preferred consistency or leave it naturally chunky.

Nutrition Info:

• Info Per Serving: Calories: 71 ;Fat: 5g;Protein: 3g ;Carbs: 17g .

To Die For Homemade Mayonnaise

Servings: 1

Cooking Time: 0 Minutes

Ingredients:

• 3 tablespoons coconut vinegar

• 1 teaspoon thyme leaves, dried

• ½ teaspoon garlic, granulated

• ½ teaspoon mustard, dry

• ½ teaspoon Himalayan salt, fine

• 3 large egg yolks

• 1 cup avocado oil

Directions:

1. Place the vinegar and seasonings in a 16 ounces measuring cup or quart-sized mason jar. Add gently the egg yolks and the avocado oil.

2. Insert the immersion blender into the mixture and turn it on high then move it up and down slightly until the mix is completely emulsified. Scrape all of the mayonnaise off of the blender by using a spatula and then transfer the mayonnaise to a jar or other container with a tight-fitting lid.

3. Store in the refrigerator for up to 10 days.

Nutrition Info:

• Info Per Serving: Calories: 262 ;Fat: 30g ;Protein: 1g;Carbs: 4g.

Nutritional Sauce With Tofu And Basil

Servings: 2

Cooking Time: 0 Minutes

Ingredients:

• 1 package silken tofu, 12 ounces

• ½ cup fresh basil, chopped

• 2 garlic cloves, lightly crushed

• ½ cup almond butter

• 1 tablespoon lemon juice, fresh

• 1 teaspoon salt

• ¼ teaspoon black pepper, freshly ground

Directions:

1. Combine the tofu, basil, garlic, almond butter, lemon juice, salt, and pepper in a blender or food processor then process until smooth. Thin with a bit of water if too thick.

2. Refrigerate in an airtight container for up to 5 days.

Nutrition Info:

• Info Per Serving: Calories: 120 ;Fat: 10g ;Protein: 6g ;Carbs: 5g .

Tricky Cheesy Yellow Sauce

Servings: 2

Cooking Time: 0 Minutes

Ingredients:

• 1½ cups steamed, mashed cauliflower florets and hot

• ½ cup coconut milk, full-fat

• ½ cup nutritional yeast

• 1 tablespoon unsalted butter, ghee, or lard

• 1½ teaspoons coconut vinegar

• 1 teaspoon Himalayan salt, fine

• 1 teaspoon garlic powder

Directions:

1. Place all of the ingredients in a blender. Cover and blend on low, slowly bringing the speed up to high.

2. Continue to blend until the sauce is completely smooth. Taste for seasoning and add a little more salt and/or garlic powder if you like.

3. Store in an airtight container in the refrigerator for up to a week. Warm in a saucepan on the stovetop over medium heat and stir occasionally.

Nutrition Info:

• Info Per Serving: Calories: 185 ;Fat: 11g ;Protein: 11g;Carbs: 15g .

Excellent Tapenade With Green Olive

Servings: 1

Cooking Time: 0 Minutes

Ingredients:

• 1 cup pitted green olives

• 2 garlic cloves

• ¼ cup extra-virgin olive oil

• ¼ cup lemon juice, freshly squeezed

• Pinch dried rosemary

• Salt

• Freshly ground black pepper

Directions:

1. Combine the olives, garlic, olive oil, lemon juice, and rosemary in a food processor. Season with salt and pepper.

Process until the mixture is almost smooth and a little chunky is okay.

2. Refrigerate in an airtight container. The tapenade will keep for several weeks.

Nutrition Info:

- Info Per Serving: Calories: 73 ;Fat: 8g ;Protein: 6g;Carbs: 2g ;

Fresh Maple Dressing

Servings: 1 ¼

Cooking Time: 0 Minutes

Ingredients:

- 1 cup canned coconut milk, full-fat
- 2 tablespoons pure maple syrup
- 1 tablespoon Dijon mustard
- 1 tablespoon apple cider vinegar
- Sea salt

Directions:

1. Whisk the coconut milk, maple syrup, mustard, and cider vinegar in a medium bowl until smoothly blended. Season with sea salt.

2. Refrigerate the dressing in a sealed container for up to 1 week.

Nutrition Info:

- Info Per Serving: Calories: 67 ;Fat: 6g ;Protein: 1g;Carbs: 4g.

Smoothies

Minty Juice With Pineapple And Cucumber

Servings: 3 ½
Cooking Time: 0 Minutes

Ingredients:

- 1 large, ripe pineapple, skin removed and core intact
- ¼ cup mint leaves
- 1 cucumber

Directions:

1. Cut the pineapple in long strips that will fit through the juicer feed tube. Process the pineapple, adding the mint leaves in between pieces, on the proper setting of the juicer. Juice the cucumber, then stir. Serve immediately.

Nutrition Info:

- Info Per Serving: Calories: 9 ;Fat: 5g;Protein: 1g ;Carbs: 2g .

Wild Blueberry Smoothie With Chocolate And Turmeric

Servings: 2
Cooking Time: 0 Minutes

Ingredients:

- 2 cups almond milk, unsweetened
- 1 cup wild blueberries, frozen
- 2 tablespoons cocoa powder
- 1 to 2 packets stevia, or to taste
- One 1 inch piece fresh turmeric, peeled
- 1 cup ice, crushed

Directions:

1. Combine in a blender the almond milk, blueberries, cocoa powder, stevia, turmeric, and ice. Blend until smooth.

Nutrition Info:

- Info Per Serving: Calories: 97 ;Fat: 5g ;Protein: 3g ;Carbs: 16g .

Lovable Smoothie With Coconut And Ginger

Servings: 1
Cooking Time: 0 Minutes

Ingredients:

- ½ cup coconut milk
- ½ cup coconut water
- ¼ avocado
- ¼ cup coconut shreds or flakes, unsweetened
- 1 teaspoon raw honey or maple syrup
- 1 thin slice ginger, fresh
- Pinch ground cardamom
- Ice

Directions:

1. Combine in a blender the coconut milk, coconut water, avocado, coconut, honey, ginger, cardamom, and ice. Blend until smooth.

Nutrition Info:

- Info Per Serving: Calories: 238 ;Fat: 18g ;Protein: 5g ;Carbs: 16g .

Fruity One For All Smoothie

Servings: 1
Cooking Time: 0 Minutes

Ingredients:

- 1 cup packed spinach
- ½ cup fresh blueberries
- ½ banana
- 1 cup coconut milk
- ½ teaspoon vanilla extract

Directions:

1. In a blender, combine the spinach, blueberries, banana, coconut milk, and vanilla. Blend until smooth.

Nutrition Info:

- Info Per Serving: Calories: 152 ;Fat: 5g ;Protein: 2g ;Carbs: 27g.

For Advanced Green Juice

Servings: ½
Cooking Time: 0 Minutes

Ingredients:

- 3 cups spinach, 120g
- 1 Granny Smith apple
- 1 cucumber
- 1 fennel bulb
- One 1 inch piece fresh ginger
- One 1 inch piece fresh turmeric
- Freshly ground black pepper
- 1 lemon

Directions:

1. Wash all the fruits and vegetables and pat dry. Juice the spinach, apple, cucumber, fennel, ginger, turmeric, and a pinch of pepper according to your juicer's instructions. Squeeze in the lemon juice and stir. Serve immediately then garnish with another pinch of pepper.

Nutrition Info:

- Info Per Serving: Calories: 225 ;Fat: 2g ;Protein: 225g ;Carbs: 51g.

Popular Banana Smoothie With Kale

Servings: 2

Cooking Time: 0 Minutes

Ingredients:

- 2 cups almond milk, unsweetened
- 2 cups kale, stemmed, leaves chopped
- 2 bananas, peeled
- 1 to 2 packets stevia, or to taste
- 1 teaspoon cinnamon, ground
- 1 cup ice, crushed

Directions:

1. Combine the almond milk, kale, bananas, stevia, cinnamon, and ice in a blender. Blend until smooth.

Nutrition Info:

- Info Per Serving: Calories: 181 ;Fat: 4g ;Protein: 4g ;Carbs: 37g .

Fantastic Fruity Smoothie

Servings: 1

Cooking Time: 0 Minutes

Ingredients:

- 2 cups carrots, peeled and sliced
- 2 cups filtered water
- 1 apple, peeled and sliced
- 1 banana, peeled and sliced
- 1 cup fresh pineapple, peeled and sliced
- ½ tablespoon ginger, grated
- ¼ teaspoon turmeric, ground
- 1 tablespoon lemon juice
- 1 cup almond or soy milk

Directions:

1. Blend carrots and water to make a puréed carrot juice.
2. Pour into a Mason jar or sealable container, cover and place in the fridge.
3. Add the rest of the smoothie ingredients once done to a blender or juicer until smooth.
4. Add the carrot juice in at the end, blending thoroughly until smooth.
5. Serve with or without ice.

Nutrition Info:

- Info Per Serving: Calories: 367 ;Fat: 5g ;Protein: 6g ;Carbs: 80g.

Smooth Butternut Squash Smoothie

Servings: 2

Cooking Time: 0 Minutes

Ingredients:

- 2 cups butternut squash purée, frozen in ice cube trays
- 1 cup coconut milk, plus additional as needed
- ¼ cup tahini
- ¼ cup maple syrup
- 1 teaspoon cinnamon

Directions:

1. Release the butternut squash cubes from the ice cube trays and put them in a blender.
2. Add the coconut milk, tahini, maple syrup, and cinnamon.
3. Blend until smooth. Thin with water or more coconut milk if the consistency is too thick to achieve the desired consistency.
4. Pour into two glasses and serve.

Nutrition Info:

- Info Per Serving: Calories: 660 ;Fat: 48g ;Protein: 10g ;Carbs: 59g .

Tropical Strong Green Smoothie

Servings: 2

Cooking Time: 0 Minutes

Ingredients:

- 2½ cups spinach
- 1½ cups water
- 1 cup pineapple, frozen
- 1 cup mango, frozen
- ¼ cup hemp seeds
- 1 teaspoon fresh ginger, grated

Directions:

1. Combine the spinach, water, pineapple, mango, hemp seeds, and ginger in a blender. Blend until smooth.
2. Pour into two glasses and enjoy.

Nutrition Info:

- Info Per Serving: Calories: 196 ;Fat: 7g ;Protein: 7g ;Carbs: 29g .

Southern Smoothie With Sweet Potato

Servings: 2

Cooking Time: 0 Minutes

Ingredients:

- ½ cup almond milk, unsweetened
- ½ cup orange juice, freshly squeezed
- 1 cup sweet potato, cooked

- 1 banana
- 2 tablespoons pumpkin seeds
- 1 tablespoon pure maple syrup
- ½ teaspoon pure vanilla extract
- ½ teaspoon cinnamon, ground
- 3 ice cubes

Directions:

1. In a blender, combine the almond milk, orange juice, sweet potato, banana, pumpkin seeds, maple syrup, vanilla, and cinnamon. Blend until smooth.
2. Add the ice and blend until thick.

Nutrition Info:

- Info Per Serving: Calories: 235 ;Fat: 4g ;Protein: 5g ;Carbs: 43g .

Savoury Smoothie With Mango And Thyme

Servings: 1
Cooking Time: 0 Minutes

Ingredients:

- 1 cup fresh or frozen mango chunks
- ½ cup fresh green grapes, seedless
- ¼ fennel bulb
- ½ cup almond milk, unsweetened
- ½ teaspoon thyme leaves, fresh
- Pinch sea salt
- Pinch freshly ground black pepper
- Ice

Directions:

1. Combine in a blender the mango, grapes, fennel, almond milk, thyme leaves, sea salt, pepper, and ice. Blend until smooth.

Nutrition Info:

- Info Per Serving: Calories: 274 ;Fat: 4g ;Protein: 3g ;Carbs: 65g.

Salad-like Green Smoothie

Servings: 1
Cooking Time: 0 Minutes

Ingredients:

- ¾ to 1 cup water
- 1 cup spinach leaves, lightly packed
- 2 kale leaves, thoroughly washed
- 2 romaine lettuce leaves
- ½ avocado
- 1 pear, stemmed, cored, and chopped

Directions:

1. Combine the water, spinach, kale, romaine lettuce, avocado, and pear in a blender.
2. Blend until smooth and serve.

Nutrition Info:

- Info Per Serving: Calories: 180 ;Fat: 10g ;Protein: 4g ;Carbs: 23g .

Cheery Cherry Smoothie

Servings: 1
Cooking Time: 0 Minutes

Ingredients:

- 1 cup frozen pitted cherries, no-added-sugar
- ¼ cup fresh, or frozen, raspberries
- ¾ cup coconut water
- 1 tablespoon raw honey or maple syrup
- 1 teaspoon chia seeds
- 1 teaspoon hemp seeds
- Drop vanilla extract
- Ice

Directions:

1. Combine in a blender the cherries, raspberries, coconut water, honey, chia seeds, hemp seeds, vanilla, and ice. Blend until smooth.

Nutrition Info:

- Info Per Serving: Calories: 266 ;Fat: 2g ;Protein: 3g ;Carbs: 52g.

Refreshing Green Iced Tea With Ginger

Servings: 1
Cooking Time: 0 Minutes

Ingredients:

- 2 cups concentrated green or matcha tea, served hot
- ¼ cup crystalized ginger, chopped into fine pieces
- 1 sprig fresh mint

Directions:

1. Get a glass container and mix the tea with the ginger and then cover and chill for as long as time permits.
2. Strain and pour into serving glasses over ice if preferred.
3. Garnish with a wedge of lemon and a sprig of fresh mint to serve.

Nutrition Info:

- Info Per Serving: Calories: 206 ;Fat: 5g ;Protein: 2g ;Carbs: 38g .

Delightful Smoothie With Apple And Honey

Servings: 2
Cooking Time: 0 Minutes
Ingredients:
- 1 cup canned lite coconut milk
- 1 apple, cored and cut into chunks
- 1 banana
- ¼ cup almond butter
- 1 tablespoon raw honey
- ½ teaspoon cinnamon, ground
- 4 ice cubes

Directions:
1. Combine the coconut milk, apple, banana, almond butter, honey, and cinnamon in a blender. Blend until smooth.
2. Add the ice and blend until thick.

Nutrition Info:
- Info Per Serving: Calories: 434 ;Fat: 30g ;Protein: 4g;Carbs: 46g .

Pain Reliever Smoothie

Servings: 1
Cooking Time: 0 Minutes
Ingredients:
- 1 stalk celery, chopped
- 1 cup cucumber, chopped
- ½ cup pineapple, chopped
- ½ lemon, zest juice
- 1 cup coconut water
- 1 apple, chopped

Directions:
1. Take all of the ingredients except the lemon zest and blend until smooth.
2. You can add ice cubes at this point if you want it chilled.
3. Serve with a sprinkling of lemon zest.

Nutrition Info:
- Info Per Serving: Calories: 237 ;Fat: 1g ;Protein: 4g ;Carbs: 58g .

Handy Veggie Smoothie

Servings: 1
Cooking Time: 0 Minutes
Ingredients:
- 1 carrot, trimmed
- 1 small beet, scrubbed and quartered
- 1 celery stalk
- ½ cup raspberries, fresh

- 1 cup coconut water
- 1 teaspoon balsamic vinegar
- Ice

Directions:
1. In a blender, combine the carrot, beet, celery, raspberries, coconut water, balsamic vinegar, and ice and blend until smooth.

Nutrition Info:
- Info Per Serving: Calories: 140 ;Fat: 1g ;Protein: 3g ;Carbs: 24g.

Fresh Berry Smoothie With Ginger

Servings: 2
Cooking Time: 0 Minutes
Ingredients:
- 2 cups blackberries, fresh
- 2 cups almond milk, unsweetened
- 1 to 2 packets stevia, or to taste
- One 1 inch piece fresh ginger, peeled and roughly chopped
- 2 cups ice, crushed

Directions:
1. Combine the blackberries, almond milk, stevia, ginger, and ice in a blender. Blend until smooth.

Nutrition Info:
- Info Per Serving: Calories: 95 ;Fat: 3g ;Protein: 3g ;Carbs: 16g.

Fresh Minty Punch With Peach

Servings: 4
Cooking Time: 0 Minutes
Ingredients:
- One 10 ounces bag frozen no-added-sugar peach slices, thawed
- 3 tablespoons lemon juice, freshly squeezed
- 3 tablespoons raw honey or maple syrup
- 1 tablespoon lemon zest
- 2 cups coconut water
- 2 cups sparkling water
- 4 fresh mint sprigs, divided
- Ice

Directions:
1. Combine in a food processor the peaches, lemon juice, honey, and lemon zest. Process until smooth.
2. Stir together the peach purée and coconut water in a large pitcher. Chill the mixture in the refrigerator.
3. Fill four large (16 ounces) glasses with ice when ready to serve. Add 1 mint sprig to each glass. Add ¾ cup peach mixture to each glass and top each with sparkling water.

Nutrition Info:

- Info Per Serving: Calories: 81 ;Carbs: 18g ;Fat: 3g;Protein: 32g;Carbs: 5g.

Vegetarian Mango Smoothie With Green Tea And Turmeric

Servings: 2

Cooking Time: 0 Minutes

Ingredients:

- 2 cups mango, cubed
- 2 teaspoons turmeric powder
- 2 tablespoons matcha powder
- 2 cups almond milk
- 2 tablespoons honey
- 1 cup ice, crushed

Directions:

1. Combine in a blender the mango, turmeric, matcha, almond milk, honey, and ice. Blend until smooth.

Nutrition Info:

- Info Per Serving: Calories: 285 ;Fat: 3g ;Protein: 4g ;Carbs: 68g .

Mixed Berry Smoothie With Acai

Servings: 3 ½

Cooking Time: 0 Minutes

Ingredients:

- One 3 ½ ounces pack frozen acai purée
- 1 cup frozen mango chunks, 1204
- 1 cup frozen berries, 120g
- 2 cups Cinnamon Cashew Milk or Almond Milk, 480ml
- 1 to 2 teaspoons maple syrup or honey

Directions:

1. Defrost the acai pack to soften under hot water. Place the acai, mango, and berries in a blender, along with the nut milk. Start on a low setting, purée the mixture until it begins to break up, stopping and scraping down the sides if needed. Slowly turn the blender speed to high and purée until there are no lumps for 1 to 2 minutes. Taste and blend in the maple syrup, if preferred. Serve immediately.

Nutrition Info:

- Info Per Serving: Calories: 273 ; Fat: 7g ;Protein: 8g ;Carbs: 47g .

Organic Berry Smoothie

Servings: 1

Cooking Time: 0 Minutes

Ingredients:

- ¾ to 1 cup water
- ½ cup raspberries, frozen
- ½ cup strawberries, frozen
- ¼ cup blackberries, frozen
- 2 tablespoons nut butter or seed butter

Directions:

1. Combine the water, raspberries, strawberries, blackberries, and nut butter in a blender.
2. Blend until smooth and serve.

Nutrition Info:

- Info Per Serving: Calories: 186 ;Fat: 9g ;Protein: 4g ;Carbs: 24g.

Nut-free Green Smoothie Bowl

Servings: 2

Cooking Time: 0 Minutes

Ingredients:

- 3 cups packed baby spinach
- 1 green apple, cored
- 1 small ripe banana
- ½ ripe avocado
- 1 tablespoon maple syrup
- ½ cup mixed berries
- ¼ cup slivered almonds, toasted
- 1 teaspoon sesame seeds

Directions:

1. Combine the spinach, apple, banana, avocado, and maple syrup in a blender and blend until smooth. The mixture should be thick.
2. Divide the mixture between two bowls. Top with the berries, almonds, and sesame seeds, then serve.

Nutrition Info:

- Info Per Serving: Calories: 280 ; Fat: 14g ;Protein: 6g ;Carbs: 38g .

Nutritious Spinach Smoothie

Servings: 2

Cooking Time: 0 Minutes

Ingredients:

- 3 cups baby spinach
- ¼ cup cilantro leaves
- 2 pears, peeled, cored, and chopped
- 3 cups apple juice, unsweetened
- 1 tablespoon ginger, grated
- 1 cup ice, crushed

Directions:

1. Combine in a blender the spinach, cilantro, pears, apple juice, ginger, and ice. Blend until smooth.

Nutrition Info:

- Info Per Serving: Calories: 308 ;Fat: 10g;Protein: 2g ;Carbs: 77g .

Delicate Smoothie With Green Tea And Pear

Servings: 2

Cooking Time: 0 Minutes

Ingredients:

- 2 cups green tea, strongly brewed
- 2 pears, peeled, cored, and chopped
- 2 tablespoons honey
- One 1 inch piece fresh ginger, peeled and roughly chopped, or 1 teaspoon ground ginger
- 1 cup almond milk, unsweetened
- 1 cup ice, crushed

Directions:

1. Combine in a blender the green tea, pears, honey, ginger, almond milk, and ice. Blend until smooth.

Nutrition Info:

- Info Per Serving: Calories: 208 ;Fat: 2g ;Protein: 1g ;Carbs: 51g.

Avocado Smoothie With Chocolate

Servings: 2

Cooking Time: 0 Minutes

Ingredients:

- 1 cup almond milk, unsweetened
- 1 cup kale, shredded
- ½ avocado
- ½ banana
- 2 tablespoons carob powder
- 1 tablespoon coconut oil
- 1 tablespoon raw honey
- 1 teaspoon pure vanilla extract
- 4 ice cubes

Directions:

1. Combine in a blender the almond milk, kale, avocado, banana, carob powder, coconut oil, honey, and vanilla. Blend until smooth.
2. Add the ice and blend until thick.

Nutrition Info:

- Info Per Serving: Calories: 295 ;Fat: 19g ;Protein: 3g ;Carbs: 27g.

Light Super Green Smoothie

Servings: 1

Cooking Time: 0 Minutes

Ingredients:

- 1 cup packed spinach
- ½ cucumber, peeled
- ½ pear
- ¼ avocado
- 1 teaspoon raw honey or maple syrup
- 1 cup almond milk, unsweetened
- 2 mint leaves
- Pinch salt
- ½ lemon
- Ice

Directions:

1. Combine in a blender the spinach, cucumber, pear, avocado, honey, almond milk, mint leaves, salt, 1 or 2 squeezes of lemon juice, and the ice. Blend until smooth.

Nutrition Info:

- Info Per Serving: Calories: 248 ;Fat: 14g ;Protein: 5g ;Carbs: 33g .

Fancy Cold Soup Smoothie

Servings: 1

Cooking Time: 15 Minutes

Ingredients:

- Frozen Veggie Mix:
- 2 cups butternut squash, diced
- 1 cup broccoli florets
- 1 cup onions, diced
- 4 cloves garlic, peeled
- 3 cups water
- Smoothie:
- 1 bag steamed and then frozen mixed veggies
- 1½ cups bone broth or water
- 2 tablespoons collagen peptides
- 1 tablespoon MCT oil or MCT oil powder
- 2 teaspoons apple cider vinegar
- ½ teaspoon thyme or oregano, dried
- ½ teaspoon Himalayan salt, fine
- ½ teaspoon turmeric powder

Directions:

1. Make the frozen veggie mix. Place all of the veggies in a large skillet with a tight-fitting lid. Add the water and bring to a boil. Cover and steam for 15 minutes or until the butternut squash is fork-tender. Remove from the heat, drain, and let cool.
2. Divide the cooled vegetables into five resealable plastic bags, about 1 cup per bag. Seal and pop in the freezer for 1 hour before making your smoothie.
3. Place 1 bag of frozen veggies in a blender when you're ready to make a smoothie and add the smoothie ingredients then blend until smooth. Drink. Store any leftovers in the fridge in an airtight container for up to 4 days.

Nutrition Info:

- Info Per Serving: Calories: 304 ;Fat: 18g ;Protein: 20g;Carbs: 9g.

Stomach Soothing Smoothie With Green Apple

Servings: 1
Cooking Time: 0 Minutes
Ingredients:

- ½ cup coconut water
- 1 green apple, cored, seeded, and quartered
- 1 cup spinach
- ¼ lemon, seeded
- ½ cucumber, peeled and seeded
- 2 teaspoons raw honey, or maple syrup
- Ice

Directions:

1. Combine the coconut water, apple, spinach, lemon, cucumber, honey, and ice in a blender then blend until smooth.

Nutrition Info:

- Info Per Serving: Calories: 176 ;Fat: 1g ;Protein: 2g ;Carbs: 41g .

For Beginners Juice With Granny Smith Apples

Servings: 4 ¼
Cooking Time: 0 Minutes
Ingredients:

- 2 celery stalks
- 2 Granny Smith apples
- 2 cucumbers
- 2 hearts romaine lettuce
- 1 bunch lacinato kale, stems removed
- ½ bunch parsley
- One 1 inch piece fresh ginger
- 1 lemon or lime

Directions:

1. Wash all the fruits and vegetables and pat dry. Juice the celery, apples, cucumbers, lettuce, kale, parsley, and ginger according to your juicer's instructions. Squeeze in the lemon juice and stir. Serve immediately.

Nutrition Info:

- Info Per Serving: Calories: 204 ;Fat: 12g;Protein: 1g ;Carbs: 15g .

Salads

Millet Salad With Olives & Cherries

Servings: 4

Cooking Time: 40 Minutes

Ingredients:

- ½ cup toasted pecans, chopped
- 1 cup millet
- 1 can navy beans
- 1 celery stalk, chopped
- 1 carrot, shredded
- 3 green onions, minced
- ½ cup chopped green olives
- ½ cup dried cherries
- ½ cup minced fresh parsley
- 1 garlic clove, pressed
- 3 tbsp sherry vinegar
- ¼ cup olive oil
- Sea salt and pepper to taste

Directions:

1. Cook the millet in salted water for 30 minutes. Remove to a bowl. Mix in beans, celery, carrot, green onions, olives, cherries, pecans, and parsley. Whisk the garlic, vinegar, olive oil, salt, and pepper until well mixed in another bowl. Pour over the millet mixture and toss coat. Serve.

Nutrition Info:

- Info Per Serving: Calories: 590;Fat: 27g;Protein: 9g;Carbs: 71g.

Mediterranean Pasta Salad

Servings: 4

Cooking Time: 15 Minutes

Ingredients:

- ½ cup minced sun-dried tomatoes
- 2 roasted bell red peppers, chopped
- 8 oz whole-wheat pasta
- 1 can chickpeas
- ½ cup pitted black olives
- 1 jar dill pickles, sliced
- ½ cup frozen peas, thawed
- 1 tbsp capers
- 3 tsp dried chives
- ½ cup olive oil
- ¼ cup white wine vinegar
- ½ tsp dried basil
- 1 garlic clove, minced
- Sea salt and pepper to taste

Directions:

1. Cook the pasta in salted water for 8-10 minutes until al dente. Drain and remove to a bowl. Stir in chickpeas, black olives, sun-dried tomatoes, dill pickles, roasted peppers, peas, capers, and chives. In another bowl, whisk oil, white wine vinegar, basil, garlic, sugar, salt, and pepper. Pour over the pasta and toss to coat. Serve.

Nutrition Info:

- Info Per Serving: Calories: 590;Fat: 32g;Protein: 12g;Carbs: 67g.

Bean & Roasted Parsnip Salad

Servings: 3

Cooking Time: 40 Minutes

Ingredients:

- 1 can cannellini beans
- 4 parsnips, sliced
- 2 tsp olive oil
- ½ tsp ground cinnamon
- Sea salt to taste
- 3 cups chopped spinach
- 2 tsp pomegranate seeds
- 2 tsp sunflower seeds
- ¼ cup raspberry vinaigrette

Directions:

1. Preheat your oven to 390°F. In a bowl, combine parsnips, olive oil, cinnamon, and salt. Spread on a baking tray and roast for 15 minutes. Flip the parsnips and add the beans. Roast for another 15 minutes. Allow cooling. Divide the spinach among plates and place the pomegranate seeds, sunflower seeds, and roasted parsnips and beans. Sprinkle with raspberry vinaigrette and serve.

Nutrition Info:

- Info Per Serving: Calories: 300;Fat: 12g;Protein: 8g;Carbs: 45g.

Tropical Salad

Servings: 4

Cooking Time: 15 Minutes

Ingredients:

- 2 cups blanched snow peas, sliced
- ½ cup chopped roasted almonds
- ½ tsp minced garlic
- ½ tsp grated fresh ginger
- ¼ cup olive oil

- ¼ tsp crushed red pepper
- 3 tbsp rice vinegar
- 3 tbsp water
- 1 tsp low-sodium soy sauce
- ½ papaya, chopped
- 1 large carrot, shredded
- 1 peeled cucumber, sliced
- 1 shredded romaine lettuce
- Sea salt to taste

Directions:

1. Combine garlic, ginger, olive oil, red pepper, vinegar, water, salt, and soy sauce in a bowl. Add papaya, snow peas, cucumber slices, and carrot and toss to coat. Spread the lettuce on a plate. Top with salad and almonds.

Nutrition Info:

- Info Per Serving: Calories: 280;Fat: 20g;Protein: 1g;Carbs: 23g.

Nutritious Bowl With Lentil, Vegetable, And Fruit

Servings: 4 To 6
Cooking Time: 0 Minutes
Ingredients:

- 1 cup red lentils
- 2 cups water
- 4 cups cooked brown rice
- One 15 ounces can lentils, drained and rinsed
- Chicken Lettuce Wraps sauce
- 1 head radicchio, cored and torn into pieces, divided
- 1 small jicama, peeled and cut into thin sticks, divided
- 2 red Bartlett ripe pears, cored, quartered, and sliced, divided
- 2 scallions, sliced, divided

Directions:

1. Combine the red lentils and the water in a medium bowl. Cover and refrigerate overnight. Drain the lentils when ready to prepare the salad.
2. Combine the brown rice and canned lentils in a medium bowl. Stir in half of the Chicken Lettuce Wraps sauce. Let the mixture stand for 30 minutes, or overnight.
3. Divide the lentil-rice mixture among serving bowls. Top each bowl with equal amounts of the soaked and drained red lentils. Garnish each serving with the radicchio, jicama, pears, and scallions.
4. Drizzle each with some of the remaining Chicken Lettuce Wraps sauce.

Nutrition Info:

- Info Per Serving: Calories: 989 ;Fat: 31g ;Protein: 31g ;Carbs: 151g .

Fantastic Green Salad

Servings: 4
Cooking Time: 10 Minutes
Ingredients:

- 1 head Iceberg lettuce
- 8 asparagus, chopped
- 2 seedless cucumbers, sliced
- 1 zucchini, cut into ribbons
- 1 carrot, cut into ribbons
- 1 avocado, sliced
- ½ cup green dressing
- 2 scallions, thinly sliced

Directions:

1. Share the lettuce into 4 bowls and add in some asparagus, cucumber, zucchini, carrot, and avocado. Sprinkle each bowl with 2 tbsp of dressing. Serve topped with scallions.

Nutrition Info:

- Info Per Serving: Calories: 255;Fat: 21g;Protein: 4g;Carbs: 15g.

Lettuce & Tomato Salad With Quinoa

Servings: 4
Cooking Time: 25 Minutes
Ingredients:

- 1 cup quinoa, rinsed
- ⅓ cup white wine vinegar
- 2 tbsp extra-virgin olive oil
- 1 tbsp chopped fresh dill
- Sea salt and pepper to taste
- 2 cups sliced sweet onions
- 2 tomatoes, sliced
- 4 cups shredded lettuce

Directions:

1. Place the quinoa in a pot with 2 cups of salted water. Bring to a boil. Lower the heat and simmer covered for 15 minutes. Turn the heat off and let sit for 5 minutes. Using a fork, fluff the quinoa and set aside. In a small bowl, whisk the vinegar, olive oil, dill, salt, and pepper; set aside. In a serving plate, combine onions, tomatoes, quinoa, and lettuce. Pour in the dressing and toss to coat.

Nutrition Info:

- Info Per Serving: Calories: 380;Fat: 11g;Protein: 12g;Carbs: 58g.

Roasted Salad With Quinoa And Asparagus

Servings: 4
Cooking Time: 15 Minutes

Ingredients:

- 1 bunch asparagus, trimmed
- 3 tablespoons extra-virgin olive oil, divided
- 1 teaspoon salt, plus additional for seasoning
- 2 cups cooked quinoa, cold or at room temperature
- ¼ red onion, finely chopped
- 1 tablespoon apple cider vinegar
- ¼ cup fresh mint, chopped
- 1 tablespoon flaxseed
- Freshly ground black pepper

Directions:

1. Preheat the oven to 400°F.
2. Toss the asparagus with 1 tablespoon of olive oil and 1 teaspoon of salt in a large bowl.
3. Wrap the asparagus in aluminum foil in a single layer and place the pouch on a baking sheet. Place the sheet in the preheated oven and roast the asparagus for 10 to 15 minutes.
4. Mix together the quinoa, onion, vinegar, mint, flaxseed, and the remaining 2 tablespoons of olive oil in a large bowl while the asparagus is roasting.
5. Slice it into ½-inch pieces once the asparagus is cool enough to handle. Add them to the quinoa and season with salt and pepper.

Nutrition Info:

- Info Per Serving: Calories: 228 ;Fat: 13g ;Protein: 6g ;Carbs: 24g.

Refreshingly Spicy Chicken Salad With Cumin And Mango

Servings: 2
Cooking Time: 15 Minutes

Ingredients:

- 2 free range chicken breasts, skinless
- 1 teaspoon oregano, finely chopped
- 1 garlic clove, minced
- 1 teaspoon chili flakes
- 1 teaspoon cumin
- 1 teaspoon turmeric
- 1 tablespoon extra-virgin olive oil
- 1 lime, juiced
- 1 cup mango, cubed
- ½ iceberg/romaine lettuce or similar, sliced

Directions:

1. Mix oil, garlic, herbs, and spices with the lime juice in a bowl.
2. Add the chicken and marinate for at least 30 minutes up to overnight.
3. Preheat the broiler when ready to serve to medium-high heat.
4. Add the chicken to a lightly greased baking tray and broil for 10-12 minutes or until cooked through.
5. In a serving bowl, combine the lettuce with the mango.
6. Serve immediately once the chicken is cooked on top of the mango and lettuce.

Nutrition Info:

- Info Per Serving: Calories: 216 ;Fat: 9g ;Protein: 19g ;Carbs: 19g .

Ready To Eat Taco Salad

Servings: 2
Cooking Time: 30 Minutes

Ingredients:

- 1 tablespoon extra-virgin olive oil
- 2 skinless chicken breasts, chopped
- 2 carrots, sliced
- ½ large onion, chopped
- 2 teaspoons cumin seeds
- ½ avocado, chopped
- 1 juiced lime
- ½ cucumber, chopped
- ½ cup fresh spinach, washed
- 1 mason or Kilner jar

Directions:

1. Heat up the oil in a skillet on medium heat and then cook the chicken for 10 to 15 minutes until browned and cooked through.
2. Remove and place to one side to cool.
3. Add the carrots and onion and continue to cook for 5 to 10 minutes or until soft.
4. Add the cumin seeds in a separate pan on high heat and toast until they're brown before crushing them in a pestle and mortar or blender.
5. Put them into the pan with the veggies and turn off the heat.
6. Into a food processor, add the avocado and lime juice and blend until creamy.
7. Layer the jar with half of the avocado and lime mixture, then the cumin roasted veggies, and then the chicken, packing it all in.
8. Top with the tomatoes, cucumbers, and cilantro, and spinach, refrigerate for 20 minutes before serving.

Nutrition Info:

- Info Per Serving: Calories: 644 ;Fat: 38g ;Protein: 63g ;Carbs: 12g.

Out Of This World Salad With Basil And Tomato

Servings: 4

Cooking Time: 0 Minutes

Ingredients:

- 4 large heirloom tomatoes, chopped
- ¼ cup fresh basil leaves, torn
- 2 garlic cloves, finely minced
- ¼ cup extra-virgin olive oil
- ½ teaspoon sea salt
- ¼ teaspoon black pepper, freshly ground

Directions:

1. Gently mix together the tomatoes, basil, garlic, olive oil, salt, and pepper in a medium bowl.
2. Serve and enjoy.

Nutrition Info:

- Info Per Serving: Calories: 140 ;Fat: 14g ;Protein: 1g ;Carbs: 4g .

Balanced Salad With Avocado And Grapefruit

Servings: 4

Cooking Time: 0 Minutes

Ingredients:

- Dressing:
- ½ avocado, peeled and pitted
- ¼ cup lemon juice, freshly squeezed
- 2 tablespoons raw honey
- Pinch sea salt
- Water, for thinning the dressing
- Salad:
- 4 cups spinach, fresh
- 1 Ruby Red grapefruit, peeled, sectioned, and cut into chunks
- ¼ cup radishes, sliced
- ¼ cup sunflower seeds, roasted
- ¼ cup cranberries, dried

Directions:

1. Combine the avocado, lemon juice, honey, and sea salt in a blender. Pulse until very smooth.
2. Add enough water to reach your desired consistency and set the dressing aside.
3. In a large bowl toss the spinach with half the dressing. Divide the dressed spinach among four plates.

4. Top each with grapefruit, radishes, sunflower seeds, and cranberries.
5. Drizzle the remaining half of the dressing over the salads and serve.

Nutrition Info:

- Info Per Serving: Calories: 126 ;Fat: 7g ;Protein: 2g;Carbs: 16g .

Beet Slaw With Apples

Servings: 4

Cooking Time: 10 Minutes

Ingredients:

- 2 tbsp olive oil
- Juice of 1 lemon
- ½ beet, shredded
- Sea salt to taste
- 2 peeled apples, julienned
- 4 cups shredded red cabbage

Directions:

1. Mix the olive oil, lemon juice, beet, and salt in a bowl. In another bowl, combine the apples and cabbage. Pour over the vinaigrette and toss to coat. Serve right away.

Nutrition Info:

- Info Per Serving: Calories: 145;Fat: 7g;Protein: 2g;Carbs: 21g.

Ginger Fruit Salad

Servings: 4

Cooking Time: 10 Minutes

Ingredients:

- 1 nectarine, sliced
- ½ cup fresh blueberries
- ½ cup fresh raspberries
- ½ cup fresh strawberries
- 1 tbsp grated fresh ginger
- 1 orange, zested
- 1 orange, juiced

Directions:

1. Mix the nectarine, blueberries, raspberries, strawberries, ginger, orange zest, and orange juice in a bowl. Serve.

Nutrition Info:

- Info Per Serving: Calories: 80;Fat: 1g;Protein: 2g;Carbs: 19g.

Chickpea & Faro Entrée

Servings: 4
Cooking Time: 30 Minutes
Ingredients:

- ½ cup dried apricots, quartered
- 1/3 cup pomegranate molasses
- 2 tbsp olive oil
- 2 chopped green onions
- 2 tsp minced fresh ginger
- 1 cup faro
- ¼ cup golden raisins
- ¼ tsp ground cumin
- ¼ tsp ground cayenne
- 1 tsp turmeric
- 1 can chickpeas
- ¼ cup minced fresh cilantro
- Sea salt and pepper to taste

Directions:

1. Heat oil in a pot and sauté green onions, ginger, apricots, raisins, cumin, cayenne, turmeric, salt, and pepper for 2 minutes. Add in pomegranate molasses, faro, and 2 cups water. Bring to a boil and simmer for 10 minutes. Stir in chickpeas and cilantro and cook for 10 minutes. Serve.

Nutrition Info:

- Info Per Serving: Calories: 445;Fat: 11g;Protein: 7g;Carbs: 78g.

Hazelnut & Pear Salad

Servings: 4
Cooking Time: 10 Minutes
Ingredients:

- ¼ cup chopped hazelnuts
- 4 pears, peeled and chopped
- 2 tbsp honey
- 2 tbsp balsamic vinegar
- 2 tbsp extra-virgin olive oil

Directions:

1. Combine the pears and hazelnuts in a salad bowl. Drizzle with honey, balsamic vinegar, and olive oil. Serve.

Nutrition Info:

- Info Per Serving: Calories: 265;Fat: 12g;Protein: 4g;Carbs: 40g.

Bulgur & Kale Salad

Servings: 4
Cooking Time: 30 Minutes
Ingredients:

- ½ cup chopped green beans, steamed
- 1 avocado, peeled and pitted
- 1 tbsp fresh lemon juice
- 1 small garlic clove, pressed
- 1 scallion, chopped
- Sea salt to taste
- 8 large kale leaves, chopped
- 16 cherry tomatoes, halved
- 1 red bell pepper, chopped
- 2 scallions, chopped
- 2 cups cooked bulgur

Directions:

1. In a food processor, place the avocado, lemon juice, garlic, scallion, salt, and ¼ cup water. Blend until smooth. Set aside the dressing. Put kale, green beans, cherry tomatoes, bell pepper, scallions, and bulgur in a serving bowl. Add in the dressing and toss to coat. Serve.

Nutrition Info:

- Info Per Serving: Calories: 200;Fat: 8g;Protein: 5g;Carbs: 30.3g.

Fragrant Coconut Fruit Salad

Servings: 4
Cooking Time:0 Minutes
Ingredients:

- Dressing:
- ¾ cup canned lite coconut milk
- 2 tablespoons almond butter
- 2 tablespoons lime juice, freshly squeezed
- Salad:
- 6 cups mixed greens
- ½ pineapple, peeled, cored, and diced, or 3 cups precut packaged pineapple
- 1 mango, peeled, pitted, and diced, or 2 cups frozen chunks, thawed
- 1 cup quartered strawberries, fresh
- 1 cup (1 inch) green bean pieces
- ½ cup shredded coconut, unsweetened
- 1 tablespoon fresh basil, chopped

Directions:

1. Whisk the coconut milk, almond butter, and lime juice in a small bowl until smooth. Set it aside.
2. Toss the mixed greens with three-fourths of the dressing in a large bowl. Arrange the salad on four plates.
3. Toss the pineapple, mango, strawberries, and green beans in the same bowl with the remaining fourth of the dressing.
4. Top each salad with the fruit and vegetable mixture and serve garnished with the coconut and basil.

Nutrition Info:
- Info Per Serving: Calories: 311| Fat: 19g ;Protein: 5g;Carbs: 36g .

Cowboy Salad

Servings: 4

Cooking Time: 15 Minutes

Ingredients:
- 2 heads romaine lettuce, torn
- 16 cherry tomatoes, halved
- 1 peeled avocado, diced
- 1 peeled cucumber, diced
- 4 oz smoked salmon, flaked
- 4 scallions, thinly sliced
- 2 tbsp ranch dressing

Directions:

1. Place a bed of romaine lettuce in a serving bowl. Layer tomatoes, avocado, cucumber, and smoked salmon. Serve topped with scallions and ranch dressing.

Nutrition Info:
- Info Per Serving: Calories: 235;Fat: 14g;Protein: 12g;Carbs: 20g.

Chinese-style Cabbage Salad

Servings: 6

Cooking Time: 15 Minutes

Ingredients:
- 4 cups shredded red cabbage
- 2 cups sliced white cabbage
- 1 cup red radishes, sliced
- ¼ cup fresh orange juice
- 2 tbsp Chinese black vinegar
- 1 tsp low-sodium soy sauce
- 2 tbsp olive oil
- 1 tsp grated fresh ginger
- 1 tbsp black sesame seeds

Directions:

1. Mix the red cabbage, white cabbage, and radishes in a bowl. In another bowl, whisk the orange juice, vinegar, soy sauce, olive oil, and ginger. Pour over the slaw and toss to coat. Marinate covered in the fridge for 2 hours. Serve topped with sesame seeds.

Nutrition Info:
- Info Per Serving: Calories: 80;Fat: 6g;Protein: 2g;Carbs: 7g.

Summer Time Sizzling Green Salad With Salmon

Servings: 2

Cooking Time: 10 Minutes

Ingredients:
- 2 salmon fillets, skinless
- 2 cups of seasonal greens
- ½ cup zucchini, sliced
- 1 tablespoon balsamic vinegar
- 2 tablespoons extra virgin olive oil
- 2 sprigs thyme, torn from the stem
- 1 lemon, juiced

Directions:

1. Preheat the broiler to a medium-high heat.

2. For 10 minutes, broil the salmon in parchment paper with some oil, lemon, and pepper.

3. Slice the zucchini and sauté for 4-5 minutes with the oil in a pan on medium heat.

4. Build the salad by creating a bed of zucchini and topping it with flaked salmon.

5. Drizzle with balsamic vinegar and sprinkle with thyme.

Nutrition Info:
- Info Per Serving: Calories: 67 ;Fat: 6g ;Protein: 7g;Carbs: 3g .

Broccoli & Mango Rice Salad

Servings: 4

Cooking Time: 25 Minutes

Ingredients:
- 3 cups broccoli florets, blanched
- 1/3 cup roasted almonds, chopped
- ½ cup brown rice, rinsed
- 1 mango, chopped
- 1 red bell pepper, chopped
- 1 jalapeño, minced
- 1 tsp grated fresh ginger
- 2 tbsp fresh lemon juice
- 3 tbsp grapeseed oil

Directions:

1. Place the rice in a bowl with salted water and cook for 18-20 minutes. Remove to a bowl. Stir in broccoli, mango, bell pepper, and chili. In another bowl, mix the ginger, lemon juice, and oil. Pour over the rice and toss to combine. Top with almonds. Serve and enjoy!

Nutrition Info:
- Info Per Serving: Calories: 290;Fat: 15g;Protein: 1g;Carbs: 35g.

Mushroom & Wild Rice Salad

Servings: 6
Cooking Time: 25 Minutes
Ingredients:

- 2 cups cremini mushrooms, sliced
- 2 garlic cloves, minced
- 1 sweet onion, diced
- 3 cups wild rice, cooked
- 2 tbsp avocado oil
- ½ tsp dried thyme
- ½ cup vegetable broth
- ½ tsp sea salt

Directions:

1. Place the wild rice in a bowl and set aside. Warm the avocado oil in a saucepan over medium heat. Place the garlic and onion and cook for 5 minutes, stirring often. Mix in vegetable broth, thyme, salt, and mushrooms and cook for 10 minutes until the mushrooms are tender and the broth reduces by half. Stir in wild rice. Serve.

Nutrition Info:

- Info Per Serving: Calories: 145;Fat: 1g;Protein: 20g;Carbs: 5g.

Warm Collard Salad

Servings: 2
Cooking Time: 10 Minutes
Ingredients:

- ¾ cup coconut whipping cream
- 2 tbsp paleo mayonnaise
- A pinch of mustard powder
- 2 tbsp coconut oil
- 1 garlic clove, minced
- Sea salt and pepper to taste
- 2 oz olive oil
- 1 cup collards, rinsed
- 4 oz tofu, cubed

Directions:

1. In a small bowl, whisk the coconut whipping cream, mayonnaise, mustard powder, coconut oil, garlic, salt, and black pepper until well mixed; set aside. Warm the olive oil in a large skillet over medium heat and sauté the collards until wilted and brownish. Season with salt and black pepper to taste. Transfer the collards to a salad bowl and pour the creamy dressing over. Mix the salad well and crumble the tofu over. Serve.

Nutrition Info:

- Info Per Serving: Calories: 570;Fat: 57g;Protein: 13g;Carbs: 8g.

Spinach Salad With Cranberries

Servings: 1
Cooking Time: 10 Minutes
Ingredients:

- 1 cup chopped fresh cranberries
- 1 tbsp apple cider vinegar
- 2 tsp olive oil
- 1 orange, sliced
- 1 cup spinach, chopped
- 2 tsp grated ginger

Directions:

1. Combine the vinegar and olive oil in a bowl. Add the cranberries, spinach, ginger, and orange and toss to coat. Chill before serving.

Nutrition Info:

- Info Per Serving: Calories: 300;Fat: 19g;Protein: 2g;Carbs: 30g.

Quick Insalata Caprese

Servings: 4
Cooking Time: 10 Minutes
Ingredients:

- 16 oz fresh mozzarella cheese, sliced
- 4 large tomatoes, sliced
- ¼ cup fresh basil leaves
- ¼ cup extra-virgin olive oil
- Sea salt and pepper to taste

Directions:

1. On a salad platter, layer alternating slices of tomatoes and mozzarella. Add a basil leaf between each slice. Season with olive oil, salt, and pepper. Serve right away.

Nutrition Info:

- Info Per Serving: Calories: 150;Fat: 15g;Protein: 1g;Carbs: 5g.

Basil-tomato Salad

Servings: 4
Cooking Time: 10 Minutes
Ingredients:

- 3 tsp balsamic vinegar
- 2 garlic cloves, minced
- 4 heirloom tomatoes, diced
- ¼ cup basil leaves, torn
- 2 tbsp extra-virgin olive oil
- Sea salt and pepper to taste

Directions:

1. In a bowl, whisk balsamic vinegar, oil, salt, and pepper. Add the tomatoes, basil, and garlic and mix. Serve.

Nutrition Info:

- Info Per Serving: Calories: 140;Fat: 15g;Protein: 1g;Carbs: 5g.

Radish & Tomato Salad

Servings: 4

Cooking Time: 15 Minutes

Ingredients:

- 2 tomatoes, sliced
- 6 small red radishes, sliced
- 2 ½ tbsp white wine vinegar
- ½ tsp chopped chervil
- Sea salt and pepper to taste
- ¼ cup olive oil

Directions:

1. Mix the tomatoes and radishes in a bowl. Set aside. In another bowl, whisk the vinegar, chervil, salt, and pepper until mixed. Pour over the salad and toss to coat. Serve.

Nutrition Info:

- Info Per Serving: Calories: 140;Fat: 14g;Protein: 1g;Carbs: 4g.

Avocado Salad With Mango & Almonds

Servings: 2

Cooking Time: 10 Minutes

Ingredients:

- 1 avocado, sliced
- 1 Romaine lettuce, torn
- ¼ cup dressing
- ¼ cup almonds, toasted
- 1 tbsp chives, chopped
- 1 mango, sliced

Directions:

1. Share the avocado and lettuce between bowls and top each with mango and chives. Sprinkle with dressing and almonds. Serve immediately.

Nutrition Info:

- Info Per Serving: Calories: 505;Fat: 40g;Protein: 8g;Carbs: 42g.

Squash Salad

Servings: 4

Cooking Time: 20 Minutes

Ingredients:

- 2 lb green squash, cubed
- 2 tbsp olive oil
- Sea salt and pepper to taste
- 3 oz fennel, sliced
- 2 oz chopped green onions
- 1 cup paleo mayonnaise
- 2 tbsp chives, chopped
- ¼ tbsp mustard powder
- 1 tbsp chopped dill

Directions:

1. Put a pan over medium heat and warm the olive oil. Fry in squash cubes until slightly softened but not browned, about 7 minutes. Allow the squash to cool. Mix the cooled squash, fennel slices, green onions, mayonnaise, chives, salt, pepper, and mustard powder in a salad bowl. Garnish with dill and serve.

Nutrition Info:

- Info Per Serving: Calories: 365;Fat: 27g;Protein: 6g;Carbs: 29g.

Soups & Stews

Low Maintenance Vegan Minestrone With Herb Oil

Servings: 8
Cooking Time: 40 Minutes
Ingredients:

- 3 tablespoon olive oil
- 1 cup diced carrots, 140g
- ¾ cup [70 g] diced celery, 70g
- 1 yellow onion, sliced
- Kosher salt
- 2 garlic cloves, minced
- Pinch of red pepper flakes, crushed
- 4 zucchinis, diced
- 2 crookneck squash, diced
- 8 cups low-sodium vegetable broth, 2L
- Two 14 ½ ounces cans diced San Marzano tomatoes
- 1 bunch rainbow chard, stems removed, coarsely chopped
- Two 15 ounces cans cannellini beans, rinsed and drained
- Herb Oil:
- ¼ teaspoon kosher salt
- 2 garlic cloves, peeled
- ½ cup extra-virgin olive oil, 120ml
- ½ cup packed herbs

Directions:

1. Warm the olive oil in a large stockpot or Dutch oven over medium heat. Add the carrots, celery, onion, and ½ teaspoon salt and cook while stirring frequently until tender for 10 minutes. Add the tomato paste (if using), garlic, and red pepper flakes, and cook until the paste turns brick red for a minute. Add the zucchini and squash and cook for 1 minute. Stir in the broth and tomatoes, bring to a boil over high heat, then turn the heat to medium-low and simmer uncovered for 15 minutes. Stir in the chard and simmer for 5 minutes longer. For 3 minutes, stir in the beans and warm them. Season with salt.
2. Make the herb oil by placing the salt and garlic in a small food processor or blender and process until the garlic is minced for 20 seconds. Add the olive oil and herbs and blend until the oil is bright green for 20 seconds.
3. Fill each bowl with soup and drizzle with 2 teaspoons of herb oil to serve.

Nutrition Info:

- Info Per Serving: Calories: 186 ;Fat: 12g ;Protein: 4g ;Carbs: 18g .

Cayenne Pumpkin Soup

Servings: 6
Cooking Time: 55 Minutes
Ingredients:

- 1 pumpkin, sliced
- 3 tbsp extra-virgin olive oil
- 1 tsp sea salt
- 2 red bell peppers
- 1 onion, halved
- 1 head garlic
- ¼ tsp cayenne pepper
- ½ tsp ground coriander
- ½ tsp ground cumin
- Toasted pumpkin seeds

Directions:

1. Preheat your oven to 350ºF. Brush the pumpkin slices with oil and sprinkle with salt. Arrange them skin-side-down and on a greased baking dish; bake for 20 minutes. Brush the onion with oil. Cut the top of the garlic head and brush with oil. Add the bell peppers, onion, and garlic to the pumpkin. Bake for 10 minutes. Cool.
2. Take out the flesh from the pumpkin skin and transfer to a food processor. Cut the pepper roughly, peel and cut the onion, and remove the cloves from the garlic head. Transfer to the food processor and pour in 6 cups of water. Blend the soup until smooth. If it's very thick, add a bit of water to reach your desired consistency. Sprinkle with salt, cayenne pepper, coriander, and cumin. Serve.

Nutrition Info:

- Info Per Serving: Calories: 130;Fat: 8g;Protein: 1g;Carbs: 16g.

Green Bean & Zucchini Velouté

Servings: 6
Cooking Time: 30 Minutes
Ingredients:

- 2 tbsp minced jarred pimiento
- 3 tbsp extra-virgin olive oil
- 1 onion, chopped
- 1 garlic clove, minced
- 2 cups green beans
- 4 cups vegetable broth
- 3 medium zucchini, sliced

- ½ tsp dried marjoram
- ½ cup plain almond milk

Directions:

1. Heat oil in a pot and sauté onion and garlic for 5 minutes. Add in green beans and broth. Cook for 10 minutes. Stir in zucchini and cook for 10 minutes. Transfer to a food processor and pulse until smooth. Return to the pot and mix in almond milk; cook until hot. Top with pimiento.

Nutrition Info:

- Info Per Serving: Calories: 95;Fat: 7g;Protein: 2g;Carbs: 8g.

Lime Pumpkin Soup

Servings: 4

Cooking Time: 30 Minutes

Ingredients:

- 2 tsp olive oil
- 3 cups pumpkin, chopped
- 1 onion, chopped
- 1 garlic clove, minced
- 2 cups water
- 1 can black-eyed peas
- 2 tbsp lime juice
- 1 tbsp pure date sugar
- 1 tsp paprika
- 1 tbsp red pepper flakes
- 3 cups shredded cabbage
- 1 cup mushrooms, chopped

Directions:

1. Warm the oil in a pot over medium heat. Place in pumpkin, onion, garlic, and salt. Cook for 5 minutes. Stir in water, peas, lime juice, sugar, paprika, and pepper flakes. Bring to a boil and cook for 15 minutes. Add in cabbage and mushrooms and cook for 5 minutes. Serve.

Nutrition Info:

- Info Per Serving: Calories: 195;Fat: 3g;Protein: 29g;Carbs: 36g.

Mushroom & Bean Stew

Servings: 4

Cooking Time: 35 Minutes

Ingredients:

- 8 oz porcini mushrooms, sliced
- 1 can cannellini beans, drained
- 2 tbsp extra-virgin olive oil
- 1 onion, chopped
- 1 carrot, chopped
- 2 garlic cloves, minced
- 1 red bell pepper, chopped

- ½ cup capers
- 1 zucchini, chopped
- 1 can diced tomatoes
- 1 cup vegetable broth
- Sea salt and pepper to taste
- 3 cups fresh baby spinach
- ½ tsp dried basil

Directions:

1. Heat oil in a pot and sauté onion, carrot, garlic, mushrooms, and bell pepper for 5 minutes. Stir in capers, zucchini, tomatoes, broth, salt, and pepper. Bring to a boil, then lower the heat and simmer for 20 minutes. Add in beans and basil. Simmer for 2-3 minutes. Serve.

Nutrition Info:

- Info Per Serving: Calories: 300;Fat: 8g;Protein: 9g;Carbs: 58g.

Scrumptious Sweet Potato Soup

Servings: 6

Cooking Time: 35 Minutes

Ingredients:

- 1 tablespoon olive oil
- 1 sweet onion, chopped, or about 1 cup precut packaged onion
- 2 teaspoons fresh ginger, grated
- 8 cups Herbed Chicken Bone Broth
- 2 pounds sweet potatoes about 4, peeled and diced, or 6 cups precut packaged sweet potatoes
- 1 carrot, diced, or ¾ cup precut packaged carrots
- ¼ cup maple syrup, pure
- 1 teaspoon cinnamon, ground
- ¼ teaspoon nutmeg, ground
- 1 cup coconut cream, plus 1 tablespoon
- Sea salt

Directions:

1. Place a large stockpot over medium-high heat and add the olive oil.

2. Add the onion and ginger. Sauté for about 3 minutes or until softened.

3. Stir in the chicken broth, sweet potatoes, carrot, maple syrup, cinnamon, and nutmeg. Bring the soup to a boil. Reduce the heat to low and simmer for about 30 minutes, or until the vegetables are tender.

4. Purée the soup in a food processor until very smooth and work in batches. Transfer the soup back to the pot.

5. Stir in the coconut cream and reheat the soup.

6. Season with sea salt, drizzle with coconut cream, garnish with a fresh herb of your choice, and serve.

Nutrition Info:

- Info Per Serving: Calories: 353 ;Fat: 13g ;Protein: 5g;Carbs: 58g .

Vegetable Chili

Servings: 4

Cooking Time: 30 Minutes

Ingredients:

- 1 onion, chopped
- 1 cup vegetable broth
- 2 garlic cloves, minced
- 1 turnip, cubed
- 1 carrot, chopped
- 2 tsp olive oil
- 1 can tomatoes
- 1 tbsp tomato paste
- 1 can chickpeas
- 1 tsp chili powder
- Sea salt and pepper to taste
- ¼ cup parsley, chopped

Directions:

1. Heat oil in a pot over medium heat. Place in onion and garlic and sauté for 3 minutes. Add in turnip, carrot, tomatoes, broth, tomato paste, chickpeas, and chili; season. Simmer for 20 minutes. Top with parsley. Serve.

Nutrition Info:

- Info Per Serving: Calories: 180;Fat: 5g;Protein: 7g;Carbs: 30g.

Green Lentil Stew

Servings: 4

Cooking Time: 30 Minutes

Ingredients:

- 2 tbsp extra-virgin olive oil
- 3 tomatoes, chopped
- 1 cup green lentils
- 1 carrot, sliced
- 1 onion, chopped
- 3 garlic cloves, sliced
- 2 celery sticks, diced
- 3 cups vegetable broth
- 1 tbsp parsley, chopped
- Sea salt and pepper to taste

Directions:

1. Warm the olive oil in a pot over medium heat. Add the onion, garlic, celery, and carrot and cook for 5 minutes until softened. Pour in tomatoes, lentils, 1 cup of water, and vegetable broth. Bring to a boil, cover, and simmer for 20-25

minutes until the lentils are tender. Taste and adjust the seasonings. Garnish with parsley and enjoy!

Nutrition Info:

- Info Per Serving: Calories: 242;Fat: 5g;Protein: 10g;Carbs: 20g.

Homemade Succotash Stew

Servings: 4

Cooking Time: 30 Minutes

Ingredients:

- 1 cup canned chickpeas
- 2 tbsp extra-virgin olive oil
- 1 onion, chopped
- 2 carrots, sliced
- 1 can diced tomatoes
- 16 oz frozen succotash
- 2 cups vegetable broth
- 2 tsp low-sodium soy sauce
- 1 tsp dry mustard
- ½ tsp dried thyme
- ½ tsp ground allspice
- ¼ tsp cayenne pepper
- Sea salt and pepper to taste

Directions:

1. Heat oil in a saucepan. Place in onion and sauté for 3 minutes. Stir in chickpeas, carrots, tomatoes, succotash, broth, soy sauce, mustard, sugar, thyme, allspice, and cayenne pepper. Sprinkle with salt and pepper. Bring to a boil and simmer for 20 minutes. Serve hot and enjoy!

Nutrition Info:

- Info Per Serving: Calories: 390;Fat: 12g;Protein: 16g;Carbs: 59g.

Cauliflower & Leek Soup

Servings: 4

Cooking Time: 25 Minutes

Ingredients:

- 2 tbsp extra-virgin olive oil
- 3 leeks, thinly sliced
- 10 oz cauliflower florets
- 4 cups vegetable stock
- Sea salt and pepper to taste
- 3 tbsp chopped fresh chives

Directions:

1. Heat the oil in a pot over medium heat. Place the leeks and sauté for 5 minutes. Add in broccoli, stock, salt, and pepper and cook for 10 minutes. Blend the soup until puréed in a food processor. Top with chives and serve.

Nutrition Info:

- Info Per Serving: Calories: 130;Fat: 7g;Protein: 3g;Carbs: 16g.

Beef-farro Stew

Servings: 4

Cooking Time: 50 Minutes

Ingredients:

- 1 can diced tomatoes
- 1 lb ground beef
- 1 medium onion, chopped
- 2 cups beef broth
- 2/3 cup farro
- 2 tbsp extra-virgin olive oil
- Sea salt and pepper to taste
- 1 cup chopped carrots
- 2 cups broccoli florets
- ½ tsp dried oregano leaves

Directions:

1. Warm the olive oil in a saucepan over medium heat. Add the beef and onion and stir-fry for 7-8 minutes until the beef is brown. Add the remaining ingredients except for the broccoli. Cover and cook for 20 minutes. Stir in broccoli and continue cooking for another 10-15 minutes or until barley is tender. Serve and enjoy!

Nutrition Info:

- Info Per Serving: Calories: 300;Fat: 13g;Protein: 3g;Carbs: 13g.

Zuppa Italiana

Servings: 6

Cooking Time: 30 Minutes

Ingredients:

- 3 tbsp extra-virgin olive oil
- 2 cups vegetable broth
- ¼ cup tomato paste
- 1 small onion, chopped
- 3 garlic cloves, chopped
- 1 tsp dried basil
- 1 tsp dried oregano
- Sea salt and pepper to taste
- ¼ tsp chili powder
- ⅛ tsp dried thyme
- 2 cans diced tomatoes
- ½ cup plain yogurt

Directions:

1. Warm the olive oil in a large pot over medium heat and sauté the onion and garlic for 5 minutes. Stir in the basil, oregano, salt, chili powder, pepper, and thyme. Add the tomatoes, broth, and tomato paste, and stir to combine. Bring to a simmer, turn the heat to low, and cook for 5-10 minutes. Remove the pot from the heat. With an immersion blender, purée the mixture in the pot until you have the desired consistency. Add the yogurt. Blend for 1 minute more. Serve immediately.

Nutrition Info:

- Info Per Serving: Calories: 80;Fat: 3g;Protein: 3g;Carbs: 10g.

Fennel & Parsnip Bisque

Servings: 6

Cooking Time: 30 Minutes

Ingredients:

- 1 tbsp extra-virgin olive oil
- 2 green onions, chopped
- ½ fennel bulb, sliced
- 2 large carrots, shredded
- 2 parsnips, shredded
- 1 turnip, chopped
- 2 garlic cloves, minced
- ½ tsp dried thyme
- ¼ tsp dried marjoram
- 6 cups vegetable broth
- 1 cup plain soy milk
- 1 tbsp minced fresh parsley

Directions:

1. Heat the oil in a pot over medium heat. Place in green onions, fennel, carrots, parsnips, turnip, and garlic. Sauté for 5 minutes until softened. Add in thyme, marjoram, and broth. Bring to a boil, lower the heat, and simmer for 20 minutes. Transfer to a blender and pulse the soup until smooth. Mix in soy milk. Top with parsley to serve.

Nutrition Info:

- Info Per Serving: Calories: 115;Fat: 3g;Protein: 2g;Carbs: 20g.

Gingery Soup With Carrots & Celery

Servings: 6

Cooking Time: 40 Minutes

Ingredients:

- 3 tbsp extra-virgin olive oil
- 2 celery stalks, chopped
- 2 carrots, chopped
- 2 onions, chopped
- ½-inch piece ginger, sliced
- Sea salt to taste

- 2 cups coconut milk
- 4 scallions, chopped

Directions:

1. Warm the olive oil in a large pot over medium heat and sauté the celery, carrots, onions, ginger, and salt for 5 minutes or until tender. Add 5 cups of water and bring to a boil. Reduce the heat and simmer for 20 minutes. Pour the soup into a blender and pulse until creamy and smooth. Stir in coconut milk. Top with scallions to serve.

Nutrition Info:

- Info Per Serving: Calories: 230;Fat: 20g;Protein: 3g;Carbs: 15g.

Curry Soup With Butternut Squash And Coconut

Servings: 4 To 6

Cooking Time: 4 Hours

Ingredients:

- 2 tablespoons coconut oil
- 1 pound butternut squash, peeled and cut into 1-inch cubes
- 1 small head cauliflower, cut into 1-inch pieces
- 1 onion, sliced
- 1 tablespoon curry powder
- ½ cup no-added-sugar apple juice
- 4 cups vegetable broth
- 1 can coconut milk, 13 ½ ounces
- 1 teaspoon salt
- ¼ teaspoon white pepper, freshly ground
- ¼ cup chopped fresh cilantro, divided

Directions:

1. Combine the coconut oil, butternut squash, cauliflower, onion, curry powder, apple juice, vegetable broth, coconut milk, salt, and white pepper in the slower cooker. Set on high for 4 hours.

2. Before serving, purée it in a blender.

3. Garnish with cilantro.

Nutrition Info:

- Info Per Serving: Calories: 416 ;Fat: 31g ;Protein: 10g ;Carbs: 30g .

Soulful Roasted Vegetable Soup

Servings: 2

Cooking Time: 30 Minutes

Ingredients:

- 2 medium carrots, peeled
- 1 cup baby Brussels sprouts
- 1 rib celery

- ¼ medium head cabbage
- 2 teaspoons fine Himalayan salt, divided
- 2 tablespoons coconut oil
- 2 cups bone broth
- ½ medium Hass avocado, peeled, pitted, and sliced
- 1 green onion, minced
- 4 sprigs fresh cilantro, minced

Directions:

1. Preheat the oven to 400°F.

2. Cut all of the vegetables into small pieces and spread them out on a sheet pan. Sprinkle with 1 teaspoon of the salt and toss with the coconut oil. For 30 minutes, roast.

3. Heat the broth in a saucepan while the vegetables are roasting over medium heat.

4. Divide the vegetables between two serving bowls when they are ready. Add the avocado, green onion, and cilantro, and sprinkle in the remaining teaspoon of salt. Divide the broth between the bowls.

5. Serve immediately. Store leftovers in an airtight container in the fridge for up to 4 days.

Nutrition Info:

- Info Per Serving: Calories: 276 ;Fat: 23g ;Protein: 6g;Carbs: 19g .s

Tomato Soup With Sweet Potatoes

Servings: 4

Cooking Time: 8 Hours 15 Minutes

Ingredients:

- 2 sweet potatoes, chopped
- 4 cups vegetable broth
- 1 can diced tomatoes
- 1 medium onion, diced
- 1 jalapeño pepper, diced
- ½ cup almond butter
- ½ tsp sea salt
- ½ tsp garlic powder
- ½ tsp ground turmeric
- ½ tsp ground ginger
- ¼ tsp ground nutmeg
- ½ cup coconut milk

Directions:

1. Pour the broth, tomatoes, sweet potatoes, onion, jalapeño, almond butter, salt, garlic powder, turmeric, ginger and cinnamon into your slow cooker. Cover with the lid and set to "Low". Cook for 8 hours. Stir in the coconut milk after cooking. Using an immersion blender, purée the soup until smooth. Serve and enjoy!

Nutrition Info:

Cold Soup With Coconut And Avocado

Servings: 6

Cooking Time: 0 Minutes

Ingredients:

- 3 ripe avocados, peeled and pitted
- ¼ red onion, chopped, or about ¼ cup precut packaged onion
- 1 cup Herbed Chicken Bone Broth
- 1 tablespoon lemon juice, freshly squeezed
- 1 garlic clove, crushed
- 1 teaspoon fresh ginger, grated
- ½ teaspoon chopped fresh dill, plus fresh dill sprigs
- 2 cups canned coconut milk, full-fat
- Sea salt
- Freshly ground black pepper
- Sliced radishes

Directions:

1. Coarsely chop three of the four avocado halves. Dice the remaining half and set it aside for garnish.
2. Combine the chopped avocado, onion, chicken broth, lemon juice, garlic, ginger, and chopped dill in a food processor. Purée until very smooth. Transfer the avocado soup to a lidded container.
3. Whisk in the coconut milk.
4. Season with sea salt and pepper. Chill the soup for at least 1 hour.
5. Garnish with the diced avocado, radishes, and dill sprigs just before serving.

Nutrition Info:

- Info Per Serving: Calories: 395 ;Fat: 39g ;Protein: 4g;Carbs: 14g .

Chickpea & Vegetable Soup

Servings: 5

Cooking Time: 35 Minutes

Ingredients:

- 2 tbsp extra-virgin olive oil
- 1 onion, chopped
- 1 carrot, chopped
- 1 celery stalk, chopped
- 1 eggplant, chopped
- 1 can diced tomatoes
- 2 tbsp tomato paste
- 1 can chickpeas

- 2 tsp smoked paprika
- 1 tsp ground cumin
- 1 tsp za'atar spice
- ¼ tsp cayenne pepper
- 6 cups vegetable broth
- 4 oz whole-wheat vermicelli

Directions:

1. Heat oil in a pot over medium heat. Sauté the onion, carrot, and celery for 5 minutes. Add the eggplant, tomatoes, tomato paste, chickpeas, paprika, cumin, za'atar spice, and cayenne pepper. Stir in broth and salt. Bring to a boil and simmer for 15 minutes. Add in vermicelli and cook for another 5 minutes. Serve warm.

Nutrition Info:

- Info Per Serving: Calories: 290;Fat: 8g;Protein: 9g;Carbs: 50g.

Traditional Chicken Pho

Servings: 6

Cooking Time: 3 Hours

Ingredients:

- One 4 to 5 pounds chicken, quartered, backbone reserved
- 2 yellow onions, peeled and halved
- 2 inch piece fresh ginger, peeled and smashed
- Kosher salt
- 2 teaspoon light brown sugar
- 5 qt water
- ¼ cup fish sauce, 60 ml, and plus more for serving
- 1 pound brown rice noodles, dried
- 1 bunch green onions, green parts only, thinly sliced
- 2 cups mung bean sprouts. 120g
- Torn basil, cilantro, and mint leaves
- Lime wedges

Directions:

1. Place the chicken pieces and backbone, onions, ginger, 2 teaspoon salt, brown sugar, and water in a stockpot with at least an 8-qt capacity. Slowly bring to a boil over medium-high heat. Turn the heat to medium-low and simmer gently, uncovered, for 1 hour while skimming off any impurities that come to the surface. Add water if needed to keep the chicken covered
2. Remove the chicken pieces from the pot using tongs and transfer them to a cutting board. Remove all the meat from the skin and bones when the chicken is cool to the touch and transfer to a medium bowl. Return the skin and bones to the stockpot. Shred the meat, then cover and refrigerate until ready to serve.

3. Return the stock to a simmer and continue to cook for 1 ½ to 2 hours. Strain the stock into another stockpot using a fine-mesh sieve and cook over high heat until reduced to 12 cups for 20 minutes. Stir in the fish sauce. You can cool the stock to room temperature, cover, and refrigerate for up to 3 days.

4. Prepare the rice noodles according to the package instructions.

5. Add half of the shredded chicken to the stock and simmer until the chicken is warmed through while the noodles cook. Reserve the remaining shredded chicken for another use. Divide the cooked rice noodles among six large soup bowls and sprinkle evenly with the green onions, and bean sprouts. Ladle the stock and chicken over the noodles and finish with the torn herbs. Serve with lime wedges.

Nutrition Info:

- Info Per Serving: Calories: 554 ; Fat: 19g ;Protein: 14g ;Carbs: 83g .

Chili Gazpacho

Servings: 4
Cooking Time: 15 Minutes
Ingredients:

- 2 tbsp extra-virgin olive oil
- 1 red onion, chopped
- 6 tomatoes, chopped
- 1 red bell pepper, diced
- 2 garlic cloves, minced
- juice of 1 lemon
- 2 tbsp chopped fresh basil
- ½ tsp chili pepper

Directions:

1. Place the olive oil, half of the onion, half of the tomato, half of the bell pepper, garlic, lemon juice, basil, chili pepper, and 2 cups of water in your food processor. Season with salt and pepper. Blitz until smooth. Transfer to a bowl and add in the reserved onion, tomatoes, and bell pepper. Let chill in the fridge before serving.

Nutrition Info:

- Info Per Serving: Calories: 120;Fat: 7g;Protein: 3g;Carbs: 13g.

Easy Thai Pork Stew

Servings: 4
Cooking Time: 50 Minutes
Ingredients:

- 1/3 cup whole-wheat flour
- ½ tsp garlic powder
- 1 lb pork loin, cubes

- Sea salt and pepper to taste
- 2 tbsp extra-virgin olive oil
- 1 cup peanut sauce
- 1 cup chicken broth
- 1 tsp red pepper flakes
- ½ lb cubed butternut squash
- 1 red bell pepper, diced
- 4 oz okra, sliced
- 2 tbsp cilantro, chopped

Directions:

1. Mix the whole-wheat flour, garlic powder, salt, and pepper in a large-sized resealable bag. Add the pork and shake to coat. Warm the olive oil in a large pot over medium heat. Add the pork and brown it for 4-6 minutes, stirring often. Pour in peanut sauce and broth, scraping up any brown bits stuck to the bottom of the pot. Lower the heat and simmer for 15 minutes. Then, add the squash and cook for another 10 minutes or until pork and squash are tender. Add the bell pepper, okra, and red pepper flakes and continue to cook for 5-7 minutes. Garnish with cilantro and serve immediately.

Nutrition Info:

- Info Per Serving: Calories: 482;Fat: 29g;Protein: 35g;Carbs: 19g.

Tomato Chicken Soup

Servings: 6
Cooking Time: 30 Minutes
Ingredients:

- 1 can diced green chiles
- 3 tbsp avocado oil
- 3 garlic cloves, minced
- 1 white onion, diced
- 1 jalapeño pepper, minced
- 6 cups chicken broth
- 1 lb shredded cooked chicken
- 1 can diced tomatoes
- 3 tbsp lime juice
- 1 tsp chili powder
- 1 tsp ground cumin
- Sea salt and pepper to taste
- ¼ tsp cayenne pepper
- 1 avocado, sliced
- 2 tbsp cilantro, chopped

Directions:

1. Warm the avocado oil in a large pot over medium hea and sauté the garlic, onion, and jalapeño pepper for 5 minutes. Stir in the broth, chicken, tomatoes, green chiles

lime juice, chili powder, cumin, salt, and cayenne pepper, and season with black pepper. Bring to a simmer and cook for 10 minutes. Serve hot topped with slices of avocado and garnished with cilantro.

Nutrition Info:

- Info Per Serving: Calories: 285;Fat: 9g;Protein: 28g;Carbs: 12g.

Homemade Asian Soup

Servings: 4
Cooking Time: 25 Minutes
Ingredients:

- 7 oz buckwheat noodles
- 4 tbsp sesame paste
- 1 cup canned pinto beans
- 2 scallions, thinly sliced

Directions:

1. In boiling salted water, add in the noodles and cook for 5 minutes over low heat. Remove a cup of the noodle water to a bowl and add in the sesame paste; stir until it has dissolved. Pour the sesame mix in the pot with the noodles, add the pinto beans, and stir until everything is hot. Serve topped with scallions in individual bowls.

Nutrition Info:

- Info Per Serving: Calories: 330;Fat: 9g;Protein: 15g;Carbs: 48g.

Hot Lentil Soup With Zucchini

Servings: 4
Cooking Time: 30 Minutes
Ingredients:

- 2 tbsp extra-virgin olive oil
- 1 onion, chopped
- 1 zucchini, chopped
- 1 garlic clove, minced
- 1 tbsp hot paprika
- 1 can diced tomatoes
- 1 cup red lentils, rinsed
- 4 cups vegetable broth
- 3 cups chopped Swiss chard

Directions:

1. Heat the oil in a pot over medium heat. Place in onion, zucchini, and garlic and sauté for 5 minutes until tender. Add in paprika, tomatoes, lentils, broth, salt, and pepper. Bring to a boil, then lower the heat and simmer for 15 minutes, stirring often. Add in the Swiss chard and cook for another 3-5 minutes. Serve immediately.

Nutrition Info:

- Info Per Serving: Calories: 300;Fat: 8g;Protein: 13g;Carbs: 46g.

Shiitake Mushroom Soup

Servings: 4
Cooking Time: 25 Minutes
Ingredients:

- 8 oz shiitake mushrooms, sliced
- 2 tbsp extra-virgin olive oil
- 4 green onions, chopped
- 1 carrot, chopped
- 3 tbsp rice wine
- 2 tsp low-sodium soy sauce
- 4 cups vegetable broth
- Sea salt and pepper to taste
- 2 tbsp parsley, chopped

Directions:

1. Heat the oil in a pot over medium heat. Place the green onions and carrot and cook for 5 minutes. Stir in mushrooms, rice wine, soy sauce, broth, salt, and pepper. Bring to a boil, then lower the heat and simmer for 15 minutes. Top with parsley and serve warm.

Nutrition Info:

- Info Per Serving: Calories: 150;Fat: 7g;Protein: 2g;Carbs: 21g.

Cold Cantaloupe Soup

Servings: 4
Cooking Time: 5 Minutes
Ingredients:

- 2 tbsp matcha powder
- 2 cups cantaloupe, cubed
- 2 tbsp chopped mint
- 2 tbsp honey
- ¼ tsp ground cinnamon
- ½ cup non-fat greek yogurt

Directions:

1. Place the matcha powder, cantaloupe, honey, cinnamon ½ cup of water, and yogurt in your food processor or blender and pulse until smooth. Serve topped with mint.

Nutrition Info:

- Info Per Serving: Calories: 170;Fat: 1g;Protein: 4g;Carbs: 41g.

Beef & Enoki Mushroom Stew

Servings: 4

Cooking Time: 30 Minutes

Ingredients:

- 2 tbsp extra-virgin olive oil
- 1 tsp dried parsley
- 1 onion, chopped
- 1 ½ lb beef, cut into pieces
- 4 sweet potatoes, cubed
- 2 carrots, chopped
- 4 cups beef broth
- 1 cup diced enoki mushrooms

Directions:

1. Heat the oil in the pressure cooker on "Sauté". Add the meat and brown it on all sides. Stir in the remaining ingredients. Seal the lid and cook for 15 minutes on "Manual" on High pressure. Do a quick pressure release, then perform a quick release. Serve warm.

Nutrition Info:

- Info Per Serving: Calories: 527;Fat: 15g;Protein: 45g;Carbs: 50g.

Cold Vegetable Soup

Servings: 4

Cooking Time: 15 Minutes

Ingredients:

- 2 lb tomatoes, chopped
- 1 peeled cucumber, diced
- 1 red bell pepper, diced
- 1 cup cold water
- 1 slice whole-wheat bread
- 4 green onions, chopped
- 2 garlic cloves, minced
- 2 tbsp extra-virgin olive oil
- 2 tbsp white wine vinegar
- Sea salt to taste

Directions:

1. Place half of the tomatoes, cucumber, bell pepper, water, bread, green onions, and garlic in a food processor. Blitz until smooth. Pour in oil, salt, and vinegar and pulse until combined. Transfer to a bowl and combine with remaining tomatoes. Let chill in the fridge for 1-2 hours.

Nutrition Info:

- Info Per Serving: Calories: 155;Fat: 8g;Protein: 3g;Carbs: 20g.

Roasted-pumpkin Soup

Servings: 4

Cooking Time: 55 Minutes

Ingredients:

- 2 red onions, cut into wedges
- 2 garlic cloves, skinned
- 10 oz pumpkin, cubed
- 4 tbsp extra-virgin olive oil
- Juice of 1 lime
- 1 tbsp toasted pumpkin seeds

Directions:

1. Preheat your oven to 400ºF. Place onions, garlic, and pumpkin on a baking sheet and drizzle with some olive oil. Season with salt and pepper. Roast for 30 minutes or until the vegetables are golden brown and fragrant. Remove the vegetables from the oven and transfer to a pot. Add 2 cups of water, bring the ingredients to boil over medium heat for 15 minutes. Turn the heat off. Add the remaining olive oil and puree until smooth. Stir in lime juice. Spoon into serving bowls. Garnish with pumpkin seeds. Serve and enjoy!

Nutrition Info:

- Info Per Serving: Calories: 210;Fat: 16g;Protein: 22g;Carbs: 17g.

Desserts

Avocado-chocolate Mousse

Servings: 4

Cooking Time: 15 Minutes

Ingredients:

- 1 cup raspberries
- 2 peeled, pitted avocados
- ¼ cup almond butter
- ¼ cup lite coconut milk
- ¼ cup cocoa powder
- ¼ cup pure maple syrup
- A pinch of sea salt

Directions:

1. Place the avocados, almond butter, coconut milk, cocoa powder, maple syrup, and salt in a food processor and pulse until smooth. Spoon the mixture into individual serving glasses. Place in the refrigerator for at least 1 hour. Decorate with raspberries just before serving.

Nutrition Info:

- Info Per Serving: Calories: 270;Fat: 20g;Protein: 7g;Carbs: 24g.

Peanut Butter Bars

Servings: 6

Cooking Time: 55 Minutes

Ingredients:

- 1 cup whole wheat flour
- 1 egg
- 1 cup peanut butter
- 1 cup oats
- ½ cup 1 brown sugar
- ½ tsp baking soda
- ½ tsp sea salt

Directions:

1. Beat together the eggs, peanut butter, salt, white sugar, and brown sugar. Fold in the oats, flour, and baking soda. Press the batter into a greased springform pan. Cover the pan with a paper towel and then with a piece of aluminum foil. Pour 1 cup of water into the pressure cooker and lower the trivet. Place the pan inside and close the lid. Cook for 35 minutes on "Manual". Release the pressure naturally. Wait for about 15 minutes before inverting onto a plate and cutting into bars. Serve.

Nutrition Info:

- Info Per Serving: Calories: 560;Fat: 20g;Protein: 8g;Carbs: 60g.

Tofu & Almond Pancakes

Servings: 6

Cooking Time: 15 Minutes

Ingredients:

- 1 ½ cups almond milk
- 1 cup almond flour
- 1 cup firm tofu, crumbled
- 3 tbsp almond butter, melted
- 2 tbsp pure date sugar
- 1 ½ tsp pure vanilla extract
- ½ tsp baking powder
- ⅛ tsp sea salt

Directions:

1. Blitz almond milk, tofu, almond butter, sugar, vanilla, baking powder, and salt in a blender until smooth. Heat a pan and coat with oil. Scoop a ladle of batter at the center and spread all over. Cook for 3-4 minutes until golden, turning once. Transfer to a plate and repeat the process until no batter is left. Serve and enjoy!

Nutrition Info:

- Info Per Serving: Calories: 170;Fat: 12g;Protein: 4g;Carbs: 13g.

Tangy Yogurt With Coconut And Vanilla

Servings: 3 ½

Cooking Time: 1 To 2 Hours

Ingredients:

- 3 cans full-fat coconut milk, 13 ½ ounces
- 5 probiotic capsules
- 1 teaspoon raw honey
- ½ teaspoon vanilla extract

Directions:

1. Pour the coconut milk into the slow cooker.

2. Cover the cooker and set to high. Cook for 1 to 2 hours until the temperature of the milk reaches 180ºF measured with a candy thermometer.

3. Turn off the slow cooker and allow the temperature of the milk to come down close to 100ºF.

4. Open the probiotic capsules and pour in the contents along with the honey and vanilla. Stir well to combine.

5. Cover again the slow cooker, turn it off and unplug it, and wrap it in an insulating towel to keep warm overnight as it ferments.

6. Pour the yogurt into sterilized jars and refrigerate. The yogurt should thicken slightly in the refrigerator, where it will keep for up to 1 week.

Nutrition Info:

- Info Per Serving: Calories: 305 ;Fat: 30g ;Protein: 2g ;Carbs: 7g .

Vanilla Cranberry & Almond Balls

Servings: 6
Cooking Time: 25 Minutes

Ingredients:

- 2 tbsp almond butter
- 2 tbsp maple syrup
- ¾ cup cooked millet
- ¼ cup sesame seeds
- 1 tbsp chia seeds
- ½ tsp almond extract
- Zest of 1 orange
- 1 tbsp dried cranberries
- ¼ cup ground almonds

Directions:

1. Whisk the almond butter and syrup in a bowl until creamy. Mix in millet, sesame seeds, chia seeds, almond extract, orange zest, cranberries, and almonds. Shape the mixture into balls and arrange on a parchment paper-lined baking sheet. Let chill in the fridge for 15 minutes.

Nutrition Info:

- Info Per Serving: Calories: 120;Fat: 8g;Protein: 2g;Carbs: 11g.

Mango Chocolate Fudge

Servings: 3
Cooking Time: 10 Minutes + Chilling Time

Ingredients:

- 1 mango, pureed
- ¾ cup dark chocolate chips
- 4 cups pure date sugar

Directions:

1. Microwave the chocolate until melted. Add in the pureed mango and date sugar and stir to combine. Spread on a lined with waxed paper baking pan and chill in the fridge for 2 hours. Take out the fudge and lay on a cutting board. Slice into small pieces and serve.

Nutrition Info:

- Info Per Serving: Calories: 730;Fat: 1g;Protein: 2g;Carbs: 182g.

Pistachios & Chocolate Popsicles

Servings: 4

Cooking Time: 5 Minutes + Cooling Time

Ingredients:

- 2 oz dark chocolate, melted
- 1 ½ cups oat milk
- 1 tbsp cocoa powder
- 3 tbsp pure date syrup
- 1 tsp vanilla extract
- 2 tbsp pistachios, chopped

Directions:

1. In a blender, add chocolate, oat milk, cocoa powder, date syrup, vanilla, pistachios, and process until smooth. Divide the mixture into popsicle molds and freeze for 3 hours. Dip the popsicle molds in warm water to loosen the popsicles and pull out the popsicles.

Nutrition Info:

- Info Per Serving: Calories: 120;Fat: 3g;Protein: 6g;Carbs: 24g.

Coconut Chocolate Truffles

Servings: 6
Cooking Time:1 Hour 15 Minutes

Ingredients:

- 1 cup raw cashews, soaked
- ¾ cup pitted cherries
- 2 tbsp coconut oil
- 1 cup shredded coconut
- 2 tbsp cocoa powder

Directions:

1. Line a baking sheet with parchment paper and set aside. Blend cashews, cherries, coconut oil, half of the shredded coconut, and cocoa powder in a food processor until ingredients are evenly mixed. Spread the remaining shredded coconut on a dish. Mold the mixture into 12 truffle shapes. Roll the truffles in the coconut dish, shaking off any excess, then arrange on the prepared baking sheet. Refrigerate for 1 hour. Serve and enjoy!

Nutrition Info:

- Info Per Serving: Calories: 320;Fat: 28g;Protein: 6g;Carbs: 18g.

Coconut & Chocolate Cake

Servings: 4
Cooking Time: 40 Minutes + Cooling Time

Ingredients:

- 2/3 cup almond flour
- ¼ cup almond butter, melted
- 2 cups chocolate bars, cubed
- 2 ½ cups coconut cream
- Fresh berries for topping

Directions:

1. Mix the almond flour and almond butter in a medium bowl and pour the mixture into a greased springform pan. Use the spoon to spread and press the mixture into the pan. Place in the refrigerator to firm for 30 minutes.

2. Meanwhile, pour the chocolate in a safe microwave bowl and melt for 1 minute stirring every 30 seconds. Remove from the microwave and mix in the coconut cream and maple syrup. Remove the cake pan from the oven, pour the chocolate mixture on top, and shake the pan and even the layer. Chill further for 4 to 6 hours. Take out the pan from the fridge, release the cake and garnish with the raspberries or strawberries. Slice and serve.

Nutrition Info:

- Info Per Serving: Calories: 985;Fat: 62g;Protein: 9g;Carbs: 108g.

Vanilla Chocolate Pudding

Servings: 4
Cooking Time: 20 Minutes + Cooling Time
Ingredients:

- 3 eggs
- 1 cup cream cheese
- 2 ½ cups almond milk
- ½ pure date sugar
- 1 tbsp vanilla extract
- 6 oz dark chocolate chips
- ½ cup coconut cream
- 1 sliced banana

Directions:

1. In a large bowl, whisk the eggs with cream cheese until smooth. Pour in the almond milk into a pot and date sugar whisk again. Cook over medium heat while frequently stirring until the sugar dissolves. Reduce the heat to low and simmer until steamy and bubbly around the edges. Pour half of the almond milk mixture into the egg mix, whisk well and pour this mixture into the remaining milk content in the pot. Whisk continuously until well combined. Bring the new mixture to a boil over medium heat while still frequently stirring and scraping all the pot's corners, 2 minutes.

2. Turn the heat off, stir in the vanilla extract, then the chocolate chips until melted. Spoon the mixture into a bowl, allow cooling for 2 minutes, cover with plastic wraps, making sure to press the plastic onto the surface of the pudding, and refrigerate for 4 hours. Remove the pudding from the fridge, take off the plastic wrap, and whip for about a minute. Spoon the dessert into serving cups, swirl some coconut whipping cream on top, and top with banana. Enjoy!

Nutrition Info:

- Info Per Serving: Calories: 720;Fat: 46g;Protein: 11g;Carbs: 71g.

Blueberry Lime Granizado

Servings: 1
Cooking Time: 15 Minutes
Ingredients:

- ½ cup pure date sugar
- 2 cups blueberries
- 2 tsp fresh lemon juice

Directions:

1. Place the sugar and ½ cup water in a pot. Cook for 3 minutes on low heat until the sugar is dissolved. Remove to a heatproof bowl and chill for 2 hours in the fridge. Blitz the blueberries and lemon juice in a blender until smooth. Add in cooled sugar and pulse until smooth. Place in an ice cream maker and follow the directions. Once ready, freeze another 1-2 hours for a firm texture.

Nutrition Info:

- Info Per Serving: Calories: 650;Fat: 2g;Protein: 3g;Carbs: 164g.

Oat & Fruit Cobbler

Servings: 6
Cooking Time: 30 Minutes
Ingredients:

- 1 tsp coconut oil
- 2 tbsp lemon juice
- 2 cups peaches, sliced
- 2 cups nectarines, sliced
- ¼ cup coconut oil, melted
- ¾ cup rolled oats
- ¾ cup almond flour
- ¼ cup coconut sugar
- ½ tsp vanilla extract
- 1 tsp ground cinnamon
- A pinch of salt

Directions:

1. Preheat the oven to 425°F. Warm 1 tsp of coconut oil in a skillet over medium heat. Place the lemon juice, peaches, and nectarine and cook. Place the almond flour, oats, coconut sugar, the coconut oil, cinnamon, vanilla, and salt in a bowl and stir to form a dry dough. Pour 1 tbsp of water to get more moisture. Break the dough into chunks and scatter over the fruit. Bake for 20 minutes.

Nutrition Info:

- Info Per Serving: Calories: 195;Fat: 8g;Protein: 4g;Carbs: 16g.

Cinnamon Faux Rice Pudding

Servings: 6
Cooking Time: 25 Minutes
Ingredients:
- 1 ¼ cups coconut cream
- 1 tsp vanilla extract
- 1 tsp cinnamon powder
- 1 cup mashed tofu
- 2 oz fresh strawberries

Directions:
1. Pour the coconut cream into a bowl and whisk until a soft peak forms. Mix in the vanilla and cinnamon. Lightly fold in the coconut cream and refrigerate for 10 to 15 minutes to set. Top with the strawberries and serve.

Nutrition Info:
- Info Per Serving: Calories: 215;Fat: 19g;Protein: 4g;Carbs: 12g.

Cinnamon Pumpkin Pie

Servings: 4
Cooking Time:70 Minutes + Cooling Time
Ingredients:
- For the piecrust:
- 4 eggs, beaten
- 1/3 cup whole-wheat flour
- ½ tsp salt
- ¼ cup cold almond butter
- 3 tbsp pure malt syrup
- For the filling:
- ¼ cup pure maple syrup
- ¼ cup pure date sugar
- 1 tsp cinnamon powder
- ½ tsp ginger powder
- 1/8 tsp clove powder
- 1 can pumpkin purée
- 1 cup almond milk

Directions:
1. Preheat your oven to 350ºF. In a bowl, combine flour and salt. Add the almond butter and whisk until crumbly. Pour in crust's eggs, maple syrup, vanilla, and mix until smooth dough forms. Flatten, cover with plastic wrap, and refrigerate for 1 hour.
2. Dust a working surface with flour, remove the dough onto the surface and flatten it into a 1-inch diameter circle. Lay the dough on a greased pie pan and press to fit the shape of the pan. Use a knife to trim the edges of the pan. Lay a parchment paper on the dough, pour on some baking beans and bake for 15-20 minutes. Remove, pour out the baking

beans, and allow cooling. In a bowl, whisk the maple syrup, date sugar, cinnamon powder, ginger powder, clove powder, pumpkin puree, and almond milk. Pour the mixture onto the piecrust and bake for 35-40 minutes. Let cool completely. Serve sliced.

Nutrition Info:
- Info Per Serving: Calories: 590;Fat: 36g;Protein: 12g;Carbs: 61g.

Coconut Bars With Chocolate Chips

Servings: 6
Cooking Time: 45 Minutes
Ingredients:
- ¼ cup coconut oil
- 1 cups shredded coconut
- ¼ cup pure date sugar
- 2 tbsp agave syrup
- 1 cup dark chocolate chips

Directions:
1. Grease a dish with coconut oil. Set aside. In a bowl, mix the coconut, sugar, agave syrup, and coconut oil. Spread the mixture onto the dish, pressing down. Place the chocolate chips in a heatproof bowl and microwave for 1 minute. Stir and heat 30 seconds more until the chocolate is melted. Pour over the coconut and let harden for 20 minutes. Chop into bars. Store for up to 1 week.

Nutrition Info:
- Info Per Serving: Calories: 125;Fat: 10g;Protein: 1g;Carbs: 11g.

Milk Dumplings In Cardamom Sauce

Servings: 6
Cooking Time: 30 Minutes
Ingredients:
- 2 ½ cups brown sugar
- 3 tbsp lime juice
- 6 cups almond milk
- 1 tsp ground cardamom

Directions:
1. Place the milk in a pot inside your Instant Pot and bring it to a boil. Stir in the lime juice. The solids should start to separate. Pour the milk through a cheesecloth-lined colander. Drain as much liquid as you possibly can. Place the paneer on a smooth surface. Form a ball and then divide it into 20 equal pieces. Pour 6 cups of water into your pressure cooker and bring it to a boil. Add the sugar and cardamom and cook until dissolved. Shape the dumplings into balls, and place them in the syrup. Close the lid and cook on "Manual" for

about 4-5 minutes. Let cool and then refrigerate until ready to serve.

Nutrition Info:

- Info Per Serving: Calories: 135;Fat: 1.5g;Protein: 2g;Carbs: 12g.

Convenient Smoothie With Mixed Berry And Acai

Servings: 3 ½

Cooking Time: 0 Minutes

Ingredients:

- One 3 ½ ounces pack frozen acai purée
- 1 cup frozen mango chunks, 120g
- 1 cup frozen berries, 120g
- 2 cups Cinnamon Cashew Milk or Almond Milk, 480ml
- 1 to 2 teaspoons maple syrup or honey

Directions:

1. Defrost under hot water the acai pack to soften. In a blender, place the acai, mango, and berries along with the nut milk. Start on a low setting, purée the mixture until it begins to break up, stopping and scraping down the sides if needed. Turn the blender speed slowly to high and purée until there are no lumps for 1 to 2 minutes. Taste and blend in the maple syrup, if preferred. Serve immediately.

2. Save the leftovers.

3. Freeze leftover smoothie in ice-cube trays. Simply pop a few cubes into your blender when you're ready to make another smoothie.

Nutrition Info:

- Info Per Serving: Calories: 205 ;Fat: 5g ;Protein: 6g ;Carbs: 35g.

Sugary Dark Chocolate Chip Cookies With Walnut

Servings: 5

Cooking Time: 10 Minutes

Ingredients:

- 1 cup walnuts/pecans
- 1 cup flax meal, ground
- 2 cups rolled oats, whole grain
- 1 teaspoon cinnamon
- ½ cup wholewheat flour
- 1 teaspoon baking soda
- ½ cup whole almond butter
- ¼ cup stevia
- 1 free range egg
- ¼ cup canola oil
- 1 teaspoon vanilla extract

- 1 cup dark chocolate chips
- ½ cup tart cherries, dried

Directions:

1. Preheat the oven to 375°F.

2. Line a baking dish with parchment paper.

3. Grind the walnuts in a blender to make flour.

4. Add the other ingredients except for the almond butter, cherries and chocolate chips then process.

5. Add mixture to a bowl then fold in the chocolate chips and cherries.

6. Mix the flour mixture into the almond butter until a sticky dough is formed.

7. To spoon mini cookie shapes onto your baking tray, use a tablespoon and bake for 9 minutes before placing them on a wire rack to cool.

Nutrition Info:

- Info Per Serving: Calories: 537 ;Fat: 39g ;Protein: 17g ;Carbs: 49g .

Tasty Haystack Cookies From Missouri

Servings: 24

Cooking Time: 1 ½ Hours

Ingredients:

- ½ cup coconut oil
- ½ cup almond milk, unsweetened
- 1 overripe banana, mashed well
- ½ cup coconut sugar
- ¼ cup cacao powder
- 1 teaspoon vanilla extract
- ¼ teaspoon sea salt
- 3 cups rolled oats
- ½ cup almond butter

Directions:

1. Stir together in a medium bowl the coconut oil, almond milk, mashed banana, coconut sugar, cacao powder, vanilla, and salt. Pour the mixture into the slow cooker.

2. Pour the oats on top without stirring.

3. Put the almond butter on top of the oats without stirring.

4. Cover the cooker and set to high. Cook for 1½ hours.

5. Stir the mixture well. Scoop tablespoon-size balls out as it cools and press onto a baking sheet to continue to cool. Serve when hardened. Keep leftovers refrigerated in an airtight container for up to 1 week.

Nutrition Info:

- Info Per Serving: Calories: 140 ;Fat: 9g ;Protein: 2g ;Carbs: 14g .

Healthy Brownies With Cacao

Servings: 4 To 6

Cooking Time: 2 ½ To 3 Hours

Ingredients:

- 3 tablespoons coconut oil, divided
- 1 cup almond butter
- 1 cup cacao powder, unsweetened
- ½ cup coconut sugar
- 2 large eggs
- 2 ripe bananas
- 2 teaspoons vanilla extract
- 1 teaspoon baking soda
- ½ teaspoon sea salt

Directions:

1. Coat the bottom of the slow cooker with 1 tablespoon of coconut oil.

2. Combine in a medium bowl the almond butter, cacao powder, coconut sugar, eggs, bananas, vanilla, baking soda, and salt. Mash the bananas and stir well until the batter forms. Pour the batter into the slow cooker.

3. Cover the cooker and set to low. Cook for 2½ to 3 hours until firm to a light touch and gooey in the middle then serve.

Nutrition Info:

- Info Per Serving: Calories: 779 ;Fat: 51g ;Protein: 18g ;Carbs: 68g .

Flavourful Glazed Maple Pears And Hazelnuts

Servings: 4

Cooking Time: 20 Minutes

Ingredients:

- 4 pears, peeled, cored, and quartered lengthwise
- 1 cup apple juice
- ½ cup pure maple syrup
- 1 tablespoon fresh ginger, grated
- ¼ cup hazelnuts, chopped

Directions:

1. Combine the pears and apple juice in a large pot over medium-high heat. Bring to a simmer and reduce the heat to medium-low. Cover and simmer for 15 to 20 minutes until the pears becomes soft.

2. Combine in a small saucepan over medium-high heat the maple syrup and ginger while the pears poach. Bring to a simmer while stirring. Remove the pan from the heat and let the syrup rest.

3. Remove the pears using a slotted spoon from the poaching liquid and brush with maple syrup. Serve topped with the hazelnuts.

Nutrition Info:

- Info Per Serving: Calories: 286 ;Fat: 3g ;Protein: 2g ;Carbs: 67g .

Layered Raspberry & Tofu Cups

Servings: 4

Cooking Time: 60 Minutes

Ingredients:

- ½ cup raw cashews
- 3 tbsp pure date sugar
- ½ cup soy milk
- ¾ cup tofu
- 1 tsp vanilla extract
- 2 cups sliced raspberries
- 1 tsp fresh lemon juice
- Fresh mint leaves

Directions:

1. Grind the cashews and 3 tbsp of date sugar in a blender until a fine powder is obtained. Pour in soy milk and blitz until smooth. Add in tofu and vanilla and pulse until creamy. Remove to a bowl and refrigerate covered for 30 minutes. In a bowl, mix the raspberries, lemon juice, and remaining date sugar. Let sit for 20 minutes. Assemble by alternating into small cups, one layer of raspberries, and one cashew cream layer, ending with the cashew cream. Serve garnished with mint leaves.

Nutrition Info:

- Info Per Serving: Calories: 390;Fat: 18g;Protein: 9g;Carbs: 54g.

Poached Clove With Pears

Servings: 4

Cooking Time: 15 Minutes

Ingredients:

- 4 cups water
- 2 cups apple juice, unsweetened
- ¼ cup raw honey
- 1 teaspoon whole cloves
- ½ teaspoon whole cardamom seeds
- 1 teaspoon pure vanilla extract
- 4 pears, carefully peeled, halved lengthwise leaving the stem on one side, core removed

Directions:

1. Combine the water, apple juice, honey, cloves, cardamom, and vanilla in a large saucepan over medium heat. Bring the mixture to a boil. Reduce the heat to low and simmer for 5 minutes.

2. Add the pear halves to the simmering liquid and cover the saucepan. Simmer the pears for about 10 minutes, turning several times until they are very tender.

3. Carefully remove with a slotted spoon the pears from the liquid and serve warm or cooled.

Nutrition Info:

- Info Per Serving: Calories: 242 ;Fat: g ;Fat: 15g;Protein: 46g;Carbs: 63g.

Fruitylicious Hot Milk

Servings: 2

Cooking Time: 10 Minutes

Ingredients:

- 1 can low fat coconut milk
- 3 bananas, sliced
- 2½cup fresh raspberries

Directions:

1. Simmer ingredients for 10 minutes on a medium-low heat in a pan.

2. Whizz up in a blender until smooth.

3. Serve warm or allow to cool and add ice cubes to serve as a chilled milkshake.

Nutrition Info:

- Info Per Serving: Calories: 116 ;Fat: 5g;Protein: 1g ;Carbs: 30g .

Grain Free And Versatile Fruit Crisp

Servings: 4 To 6

Cooking Time: 30 To 35 Minutes

Ingredients:

- 3 cups mixed fresh berries
- ½ cup sunflower seeds
- ¾ cup shredded coconut, unsweetened
- ¼ cup coconut sugar
- ¼ cup coconut oil

Directions:

1. Preheat the oven to 350°F.

2. Combine the fruit in a 9-by-9-inch baking dish.

3. Mix together in a small bowl the sunflower seeds, shredded coconut, and coconut sugar.

4. Stir in the coconut oil and incorporate it throughout by using your hands.

5. Crumble the topping over the fruit.

6. Place the dish in the preheated oven and bake for 30 to 35 minutes or until the topping is golden and the fruit is bubbling.

Nutrition Info:

- Info Per Serving: Calories: 379 ;Fat: 29g ;Protein: 4g ;Carbs: 29g.

Apples Stuffed With Pecans & Dates

Servings: 4

Cooking Time: 40 Minutes

Ingredients:

- 4 cored apples, halved lengthwise
- ½ cup chopped pecans
- 4 pitted dates, chopped
- 1 tbsp almond butter
- 1 tbsp pure maple syrup
- ¼ tsp ground cinnamon

Directions:

1. Preheat your oven to 360ºF. Mix the pecans, dates, almond butter, maple syrup, and cinnamon in a bowl. Arrange the apple on a greased baking pan and fill them with the pecan mixture. Pour 1 tbsp of water into the baking pan. Bake for 30-40 minutes, until soft and lightly browned. Serve warm or cold.

Nutrition Info:

- Info Per Serving: Calories: 240;Fat: 12g;Protein: 2g;Carbs: 36g.

Appealing Blueberries, Nuts, And Honey With Greek Yogurt

Servings: 4

Cooking Time: 0 Minutes

Ingredients:

- 3 cups plain Greek yogurt, unsweetened
- 1½ cups blueberries
- ¾ cup mixed nuts, chopped
- ½ cup honey

Directions:

1. Spoon the yogurt into four bowls. Sprinkle with the blueberries and nuts and drizzle with honey.

Nutrition Info:

- Info Per Serving: Calories: 457 ;Fat: 18g ;Protein: 15g ;Carbs: 62g .

Glazed Chili Chocolate Cake

Servings: 4

Cooking Time: 45 Minutes

Ingredients:

- 1 ¾ cups whole-grain flour
- 1 cup pure date sugar
- ¼ cup cocoa powder
- 1 tsp baking soda
- ½ tsp baking powder
- 1 ½ tsp ground cinnamon
- ¼ tsp ground chili

- 3 tbsp olive oil
- 1 tbsp apple cider vinegar
- 1 ½ tsp pure vanilla extract
- 2 squares dark chocolate
- ¼ cup soy milk
- ½ cup pure date sugar
- 3 tbsp almond butter
- ½ tsp pure vanilla extract

Directions:

1. Preheat your oven to 360°F. In a bowl, mix the whole-grain flour, date sugar, baking soda, baking powder, cinnamon, and chili. In another bowl, whisk the oil, vinegar, vanilla, and 1 cup cold water. Pour into the flour mixture, stir to combine. Pour the batter into a greased baking pan. Bake for 30 minutes. Let cool for 10-15 minutes. Take out the cake inverted onto a wire rack and allow to cool completely. Place the chocolate and soy milk in a pot. Cook until the chocolate is melted. Add in sugar, cook for 5 minutes. Turn the heat off and mix in almond butter and vanilla. Cover the cake with the glaze. Refrigerate until the glaze is set. Serve.

Nutrition Info:

- Info Per Serving: Calories: 680;Fat: 36g;Protein: 10g;Carbs: 85g.

Elegant Panna Cotta With Honey And Blackberry-lime Sauce

Servings: 6
Cooking Time: 5 Minutes
Ingredients:

- 2 ½ cups canned unsweetened coconut milk, 600ml
- 2 teaspoons gelatin
- ¼ cup honey, 60ml
- 1 vanilla bean, split and seeds scraped
- Kosher salt
- Blackberry-Lime Sauce:
- 2 cups blackberries, 240g
- Finely grated zest of ½ lime, plus 2 teaspoons lime juice
- 1 teaspoon raw cane sugar

Directions:

1. In a small bowl, place ½ cup (120 ml) of coconut milk. Sprinkle the gelatin over the top and allow it to sit for 2 minutes.
2. Place the remaining 2 cups (480 ml) coconut milk, honey, vanilla bean with its seeds, and a pinch of salt in a medium saucepan. Warm over low heat while whisking until

bubbles form around the edge of the pan. Remove from the heat and let the mixture steep for 5 minutes.

3. Pour the coconut milk mixture through a fine-mesh strainer into a large bowl. Discard the vanilla bean. Whisk slowly the gelatin mixture into the warm coconut mixture until there are no lumps of gelatin. Divide evenly among six ½ cup ramekins or wine glasses. Cover and refrigerate until set for 4 hours or overnight.

4. Make the blackberry-lime sauce. In a medium bowl, place the blackberries, lime zest, lime juice, and sugar. Gently mash using a fork or pastry blender the berries, leaving some large pieces of berry while allowing some of the juices to make a sauce. Set aside for 10 minutes, or cover and refrigerate up to overnight.

5. Spoon the sauce over each chilled panna cotta. Serve immediately.

Nutrition Info:

- Info Per Serving: Calories: 357 ;Fat: 24g ;Protein: 4g ;Carbs: 39g .

Nightshade Free Cinnamon Pecans

Servings: 3 ½
Cooking Time: 3 To 4 Hours
Ingredients:

- 1 tablespoon coconut oil
- 1 large egg white
- 2 tablespoons cinnamon, ground
- 2 teaspoons vanilla extract
- ¼ cup maple syrup
- 2 tablespoons coconut sugar
- ¼ teaspoon sea salt
- 3 cups pecan halves

Directions:

1. Coat the slow cooker with the coconut oil.
2. Whisk the egg white in a medium bowl.
3. Add the cinnamon, vanilla, maple syrup, coconut sugar, and salt. Whisk well to combine.
4. Add the pecans and stir to coat. Pour the pecans into the slow cooker.
5. Cover the cooker and set to low. Cook for 3 to 4 hours.
6. Remove the pecans from the slow cooker and spread them on a baking sheet or other cooling surface. Before serving, let cool for 5 to 10 minutes. Store in an airtight container at room temperature for up to 2 weeks.

Nutrition Info:

- Info Per Serving: Calories: 195 ;Fat: 18g ;Protein: 2g ;Carbs: 9g .

30-Day Meal Plan

Day 1
Breakfast: Mediterranean Coconut Pancakes
Lunch: Scrambled Tofu With Bell Pepper
Dinner: Millet Salad With Olives & Cherries

Day 2
Breakfast: Scrambled Eggs With Smoked Salmon
Lunch: Broccoli & Chicken Stir-fry
Dinner: Mediterranean Pasta Salad

Day 3
Breakfast: Baked Berry Millet With Applesauce
Lunch: Gingered Beef Stir-fry With Peppers
Dinner: Bean & Roasted Parsnip Salad

Day 4
Breakfast: Simple Apple Muffins
Lunch: Smoky Lamb Souvlaki
Dinner: Tropical Salad

Day 5
Breakfast: Almond Flour English Muffins
Lunch: Creamy Turkey With Mushrooms
Dinner: Nutritious Bowl With Lentil, Vegetable, And Fruit

Day 6
Breakfast: Pear & Kale Smoothie
Lunch: Delightful Stuffed Lamb With Peppers
Dinner: Fantastic Green Salad

Day 7
Breakfast: Berry Quinoa Bowl
Lunch: Classic And Minty Lamb Burgers
Dinner: Lettuce & Tomato Salad With Quinoa

Day 8
Breakfast: Fruity And Seedy Breakfast Bars
Lunch: Rosemary Lamb Chops
Dinner: Roasted Salad With Quinoa And Asparagus

Day 9
Breakfast: Flaky Eggs With Cabbage
Lunch: Good For The Bones Stir Fried Sesame Chicken
Dinner: Ready To Eat Taco Salad

Day 10
Breakfast: Blueberry Muesli Breakfast
Lunch: Tomato & Lentil Lamb Ragù
Dinner: Out Of This World Salad With Basil And Tomato

Day 11
Breakfast: Almond & Coconut Granola With Cherries
Lunch: Korean Chicken Thighs
Dinner: Balanced Salad With Avocado And Grapefruit

Day 12
Breakfast: Cherry Oatmeal
Lunch: Port Wine Garlicky Lamb
Dinner: Beet Slaw With Apples

Day 13
Breakfast: Raspberry Almond Smoothie
Lunch: Mustardy Beef Steaks
Dinner: Ginger Fruit Salad

Day 14
Breakfast: Dilly Vegetable Quinoa
Lunch: Mustardy Beef Steaks
Dinner: Chickpea & Faro Entrée

Day 15
Breakfast: Strawberry & Pecan Breakfast
Lunch: Incredible Tacos With Pork
Dinner: Hazelnut & Pear Salad

Day 16
Breakfast: Coconut Oat Bread
Lunch: Grilled Beef Burgers With Chipotle Aioli
Dinner: Bulgur & Kale Salad

Day 17
Breakfast: Kale & Avocado Toast
Lunch: Worth It Glazed Chicken Thighs With Cauliflower
Dinner: Fragrant Coconut Fruit Salad

Day 18
Breakfast: Maple Crêpes
Lunch: Tangy Beef Ribs
Dinner: Cowboy Salad

Day 19
Breakfast: Sweet Potato, Tomato, & Onion Frittata
Lunch: Cumin Lamb Meatballs With Aioli
Dinner: Chinese-style Cabbage Salad

Day 20
Breakfast: Mushroom Crepes
Lunch: Italian Turkey Meatballs
Dinner: Broccoli & Mango Rice Salad

Day 21
Breakfast: Thyme Cremini Oats
Lunch: Tastylicious Chicken Cajun With Prawn
Dinner: Mushroom & Wild Rice Salad

Day 22
Breakfast: Delicious Matcha Smoothie
Lunch: Fiery Pork Loin With Lime
Dinner: Warm Collard Salad

Day 23
Breakfast: Tropical Smoothie Bowl
Lunch: Paleo Turkey Thighs With Mushroom
Dinner: Spinach Salad With Cranberries

Day 24
Breakfast: Appetizing Crepes With Berries
Lunch: Italian Spinach Chicken
Dinner: Quick Insalata Caprese

Day 25
Breakfast: Pumpkin Cake With Pistachios
Lunch: Chicken Satay
Dinner: Basil-tomato Salad

Day 26
Breakfast: Green Banana Smoothie
Lunch: Traditional Beef Bolognese
Dinner: Radish & Tomato Salad

Day 27
Breakfast: Terrific Pancakes With Coconut And Banana
Lunch: Nut Free Turkey Burgers With Ginger
Dinner: Avocado Salad With Mango & Almonds

Day 28
Breakfast: Hazelnut & Raspberry Quinoa
Lunch: Sheet Pan Baked Salmon With Asparagus
Dinner: Squash Salad

Day 29
Breakfast: Grilled Chicken Sandwiches
Lunch: Avocado & Tuna Toast
Dinner: Cayenne Pumpkin Soup

Day 30
Breakfast: Veggie & Beef Brisket
Lunch: Baked Tilapia With Chili Kale
Dinner: Lime Pumpkin Soup

INDEX

A

B

C

D

Delightful Smoothie With Apple And Honey 60
Delightful Stuffed Lamb With Peppers 23
Dilly Vegetable Quinoa 18
Distinctive Latino Stew With Black Bean 40

E

Easy Thai Pork Stew 78
Elegant Panna Cotta With Honey And Blackberry-lime Sauce 88
Excellent Tapenade With Green Olive 55

F

Fancy Cold Soup Smoothie 62
Fantastic Fruity Smoothie 58
Fantastic Green Salad 65
Fantastic On Hand Marinara Sauce 54
Feels Like Autumn Loaf With Root Vegetable 43
Fennel & Parsnip Bisque 75
Fiery Pork Loin With Lime 28
Flaky Eggs With Cabbage 16
Flavourful Glazed Maple Pears And Hazelnuts 86
For Advanced Green Juice 57
For Beginners Juice With Granny Smith Apples 63
Fragrant Coconut Fruit Salad 68
Fragrant Peach Butter 51
French Pistou 49
Fresh Berry Smoothie With Ginger 60
Fresh Maple Dressing 56
Fresh Minty Punch With Peach 60
Fruity And Seedy Breakfast Bars 16
Fruity One For All Smoothie 57
Fruitylicious Hot Milk 87

G

Garlicky Sauce With Tahini 51
Ginger Fruit Salad 67
Gingered Beef Stir-fry With Peppers 22
Gingery Sea Bass 32
Gingery Soup With Carrots & Celery 75
Glazed Chili Chocolate Cake 87
Gluten Free Apple Chutney 53
Goddess And Vibrant Green Dressing 54
Good For The Bones Stir Fried Sesame Chicken 24

Grain Free And Versatile Fruit Crisp 87

Granola Dish With Buckwheat, Berries, Apples, Pumpkin Seeds And Sunflower Seeds 14

Great On Everything Ginger Sauce 52

Green Banana Smoothie 21

Green Bean & Zucchini Velouté 72

Green Lentil Stew 74

Grilled Beef Burgers With Chipotle Aioli 26

Grilled Chicken Sandwiches 22

H

Handy Veggie Smoothie 60

Hawaiian Tuna 39

Hazelnut & Pear Salad 68

Hazelnut & Raspberry Quinoa 21

Hazelnut Crusted Trout Fillets 38

Healthy Brownies With Cacao 86

Healthy Vegan Buffalo Dip 49

Herbaceous Spread With Avocado 51

Homemade Asian Soup 79

Homemade Pizza With Lean Meat, Jalapeno, And Tapioca Starch 25

Homemade Succotash Stew 74

Hot And Spicy Scrambled Tofu And Spinach 44

Hot Bean Salad 43

Hot Lentil Soup With Zucchini 79

Hot Quinoa Florentine 44

I

Incredible Tacos With Pork 26

Italian Spinach Chicken 29

Italian Turkey Meatballs 28

J

Japanese Salmon Cakes 36

K

Kale & Avocado Toast 18

Korean Chicken Thighs 24

L

Layered Raspberry & Tofu Cups 86

Lemon Sauce Salmon 34
Lemony Honey With Ginger 49
Lettuce & Tomato Salad With Quinoa 65
Light Super Green Smoothie 62
Lime Pumpkin Soup 73
Lime-avocado Ahi Poke 31
Lovable Smoothie With Coconut And Ginger 57
Low Maintenance Vegan Minestrone With Herb Oil 72

M

Magical One-pot Tomato Basil Pasta 45
Mango Chocolate Fudge 82
Maple Crêpes 18
Marinated Greek Dressing 51
Marvellous Chocolate Chili 25
Mediterranean Coconut Pancakes 14
Mediterranean Pasta Salad 64
Mediterranean Salmon 36
Milk Dumplings In Cardamom Sauce 84
Millet Salad With Olives & Cherries 64
Minty Juice With Pineapple And Cucumber 57
Mixed Berry Smoothie With Acai 61
Mushroom & Bean Stew 73
Mushroom & Olive Cod Fillets 38
Mushroom & Wild Rice Salad 70
Mushroom Crepes 19
Mushroom Pizza 40
Mustardy Beef Steaks 25
Must-have Ranch Dressing 50

N

Natural Dressing With Ginger And Turmeric 50
Nightshade Free Cinnamon Pecans 88
Nut Free Turkey Burgers With Ginger 30
Nut-free Green Smoothie Bowl 61
Nutritional Sauce With Tofu And Basil 55
Nutritious Bowl With Lentil, Vegetable, And Fruit 65
Nutritious Spinach Smoothie 61

O

Oat & Fruit Cobbler 83
Old Fashioned Dressing With Lemon And Mustard 50

T

Traditional Chicken Pho 77
Tricky Cheesy Yellow Sauce 55
Tropical Salad 64
Tropical Smoothie Bowl 20
Tropical Strong Green Smoothie 58

V

Vanilla Chocolate Pudding 83
Vanilla Cranberry & Almond Balls 82
Vegetable & Hummus Pizza 41
Vegetable Chili 74
Vegetarian Mango Smoothie With Green Tea And Turmeric 61
Vegetarian Sloppy Joes 42
Veggie & Beef Brisket 26
Veggie Burger Patties 43
Verde Chimichurri With Parsley 52

W

Warm Collard Salad 70
Watercress & Mushroom Spaghetti 44
Wild Blueberry Smoothie With Chocolate And Turmeric 57
Worth It Glazed Chicken Thighs With Cauliflower 27

Z

Zucchini & Chickpea Casserole 48
Zuppa Italiana 75

Made in United States
North Haven, CT
13 August 2023

40272949R00054